WU ZE TIAN

624 A.D. ~

By Queenie Chan

BOOKS IN THE SERIES

Hatshepsut (Series #1)
Wu Zetian (Series #2)
Elizabeth 1 (Series #3)

OTHER BOOKS BY THE AUTHOR

The Dreaming v1-3
The Dreaming: Perfect Collection
In Odd We Trust
Odd Is On Our Side
House of Odd
Small Shen
Queenie Chan: Short Stories 2000-2010
Short Ghost Stories: The Man with the Axe in his Back
Fabled Kingdom v1-3

ISBN: 978-1-925376-08-1

Published by Bento Comics
First published in Australia
in 2019 by Bento Comics

Typeset in 8.5pt Komika Text by Queenie Chan
Cover designed by Queenie Chan

Women Who Were Kings:
Wu Zetian

Book 2

꧷꧷꧷꧷꧷꧷꧷꧷꧷꧷꧷꧷꧷꧷

By Queenie Chan

www.queeniechan.com

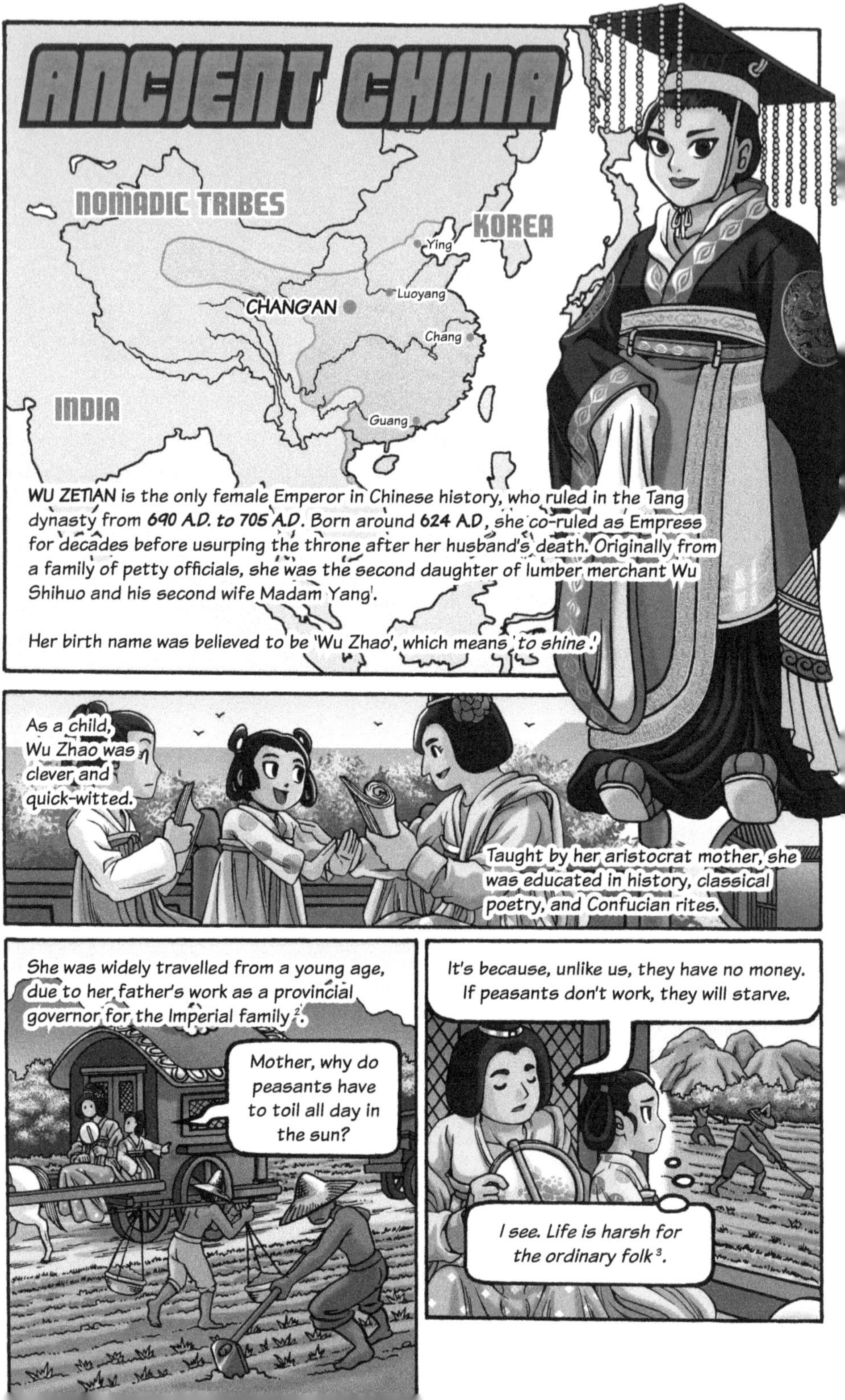
ANCIENT CHINA
NOMADIC TRIBES
KOREA
Ying
Luoyang
CHANG'AN
Chang
INDIA
Guang
WU ZETIAN is the only female Emperor in Chinese history, who ruled in the Tang dynasty from 690 A.D. to 705 A.D. Born around 624 A.D., she co-ruled as Empress for decades before usurping the throne after her husband's death. Originally from a family of petty officials, she was the second daughter of lumber merchant Wu Shihuo and his second wife Madam Yang[1].
Her birth name was believed to be 'Wu Zhao', which means 'to shine'.
As a child, Wu Zhao was clever and quick-witted.
Taught by her aristocrat mother, she was educated in history, classical poetry, and Confucian rites.
She was widely travelled from a young age, due to her father's work as a provincial governor for the Imperial family[2].
Mother, why do peasants have to toil all day in the sun?
It's because, unlike us, they have no money. If peasants don't work, they will starve.
I see. Life is harsh for the ordinary folk[3].

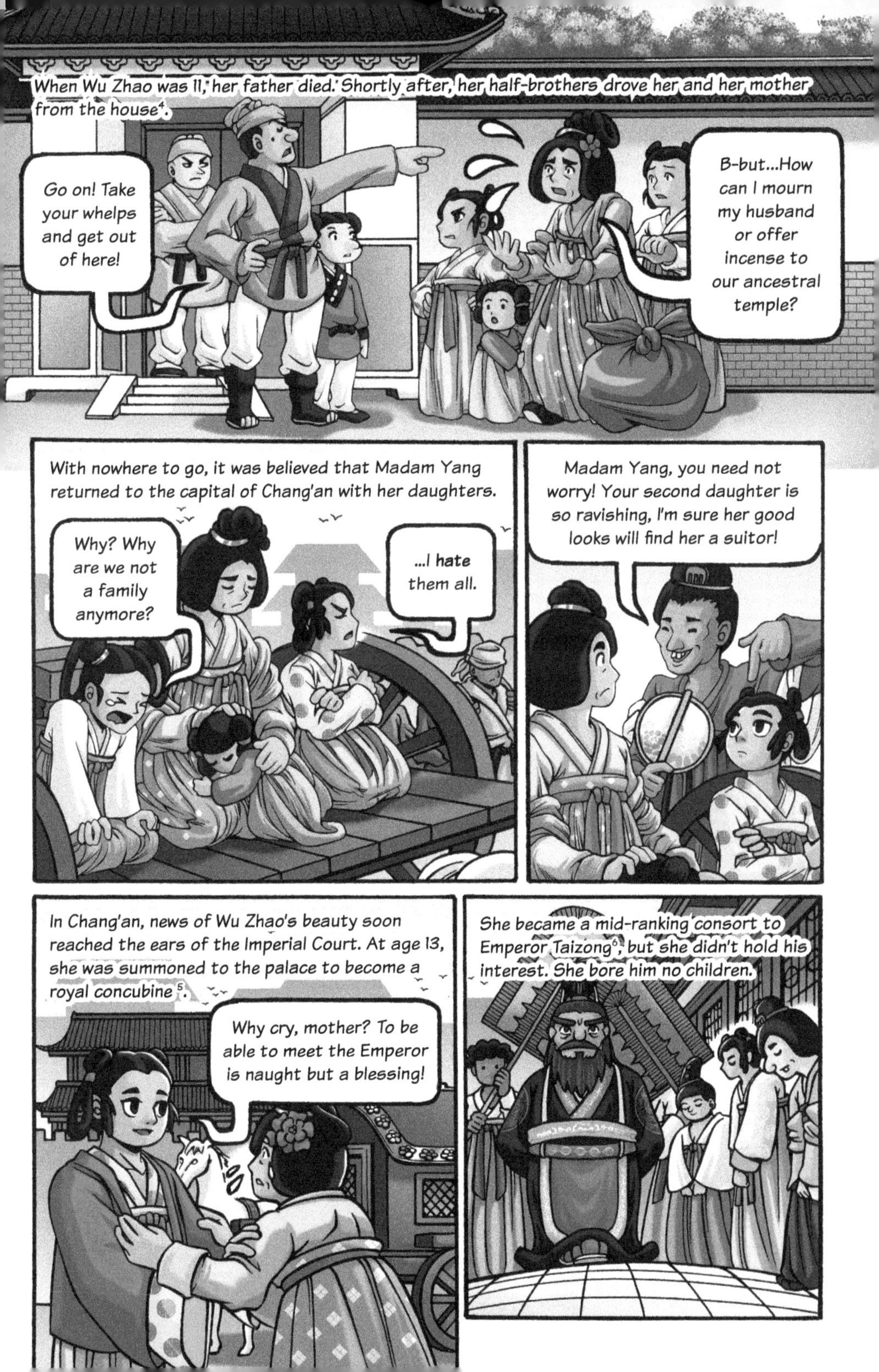
When Wu Zhao was 11, her father died. Shortly after, her half-brothers drove her and her mother from the house[4].
Go on! Take your whelps and get out of here!
B-but...How can I mourn my husband or offer incense to our ancestral temple?
With nowhere to go, it was believed that Madam Yang returned to the capital of Chang'an with her daughters.
Why? Why are we not a family anymore?
...I **hate** them all.
Madam Yang, you need not worry! Your second daughter is so ravishing, I'm sure her good looks will find her a suitor!
In Chang'an, news of Wu Zhao's beauty soon reached the ears of the Imperial Court. At age 13, she was summoned to the palace to become a royal concubine[5].
Why cry, mother? To be able to meet the Emperor is naught but a blessing!
She became a mid-ranking consort to Emperor Taizong[6], but she didn't hold his interest. She bore him no children.

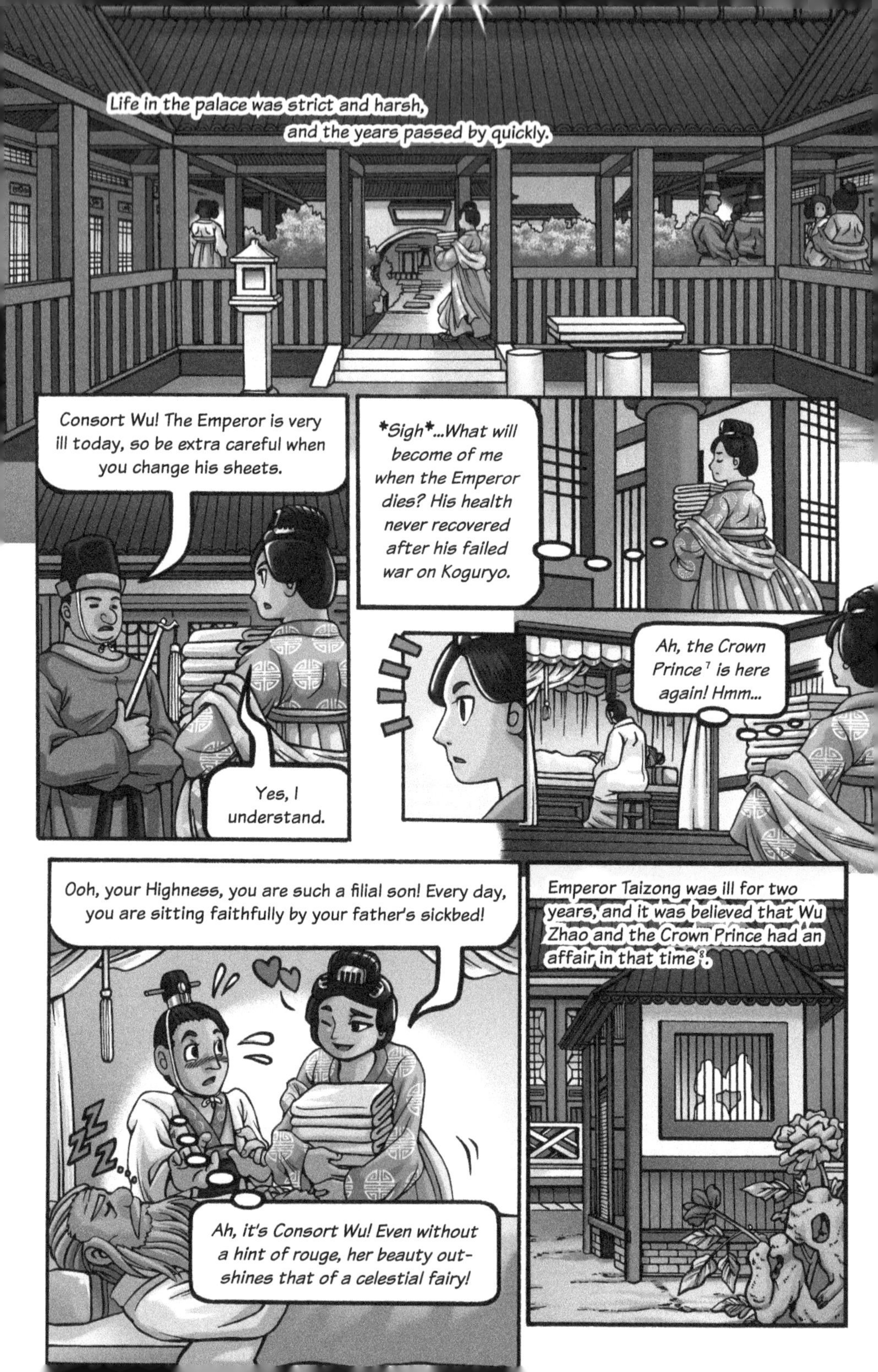
Life in the palace was strict and harsh, and the years passed by quickly.
Consort Wu! The Emperor is very ill today, so be extra careful when you change his sheets.
Yes, I understand.
Sigh...What will become of me when the Emperor dies? His health never recovered after his failed war on Koguryo.
Ah, the Crown Prince[7] is here again! Hmm...
Ooh, your Highness, you are such a filial son! Every day, you are sitting faithfully by your father's sickbed!
Ah, it's Consort Wu! Even without a hint of rouge, her beauty outshines that of a celestial fairy!
Emperor Taizong was ill for two years, and it was believed that Wu Zhao and the Crown Prince had an affair in that time[8].

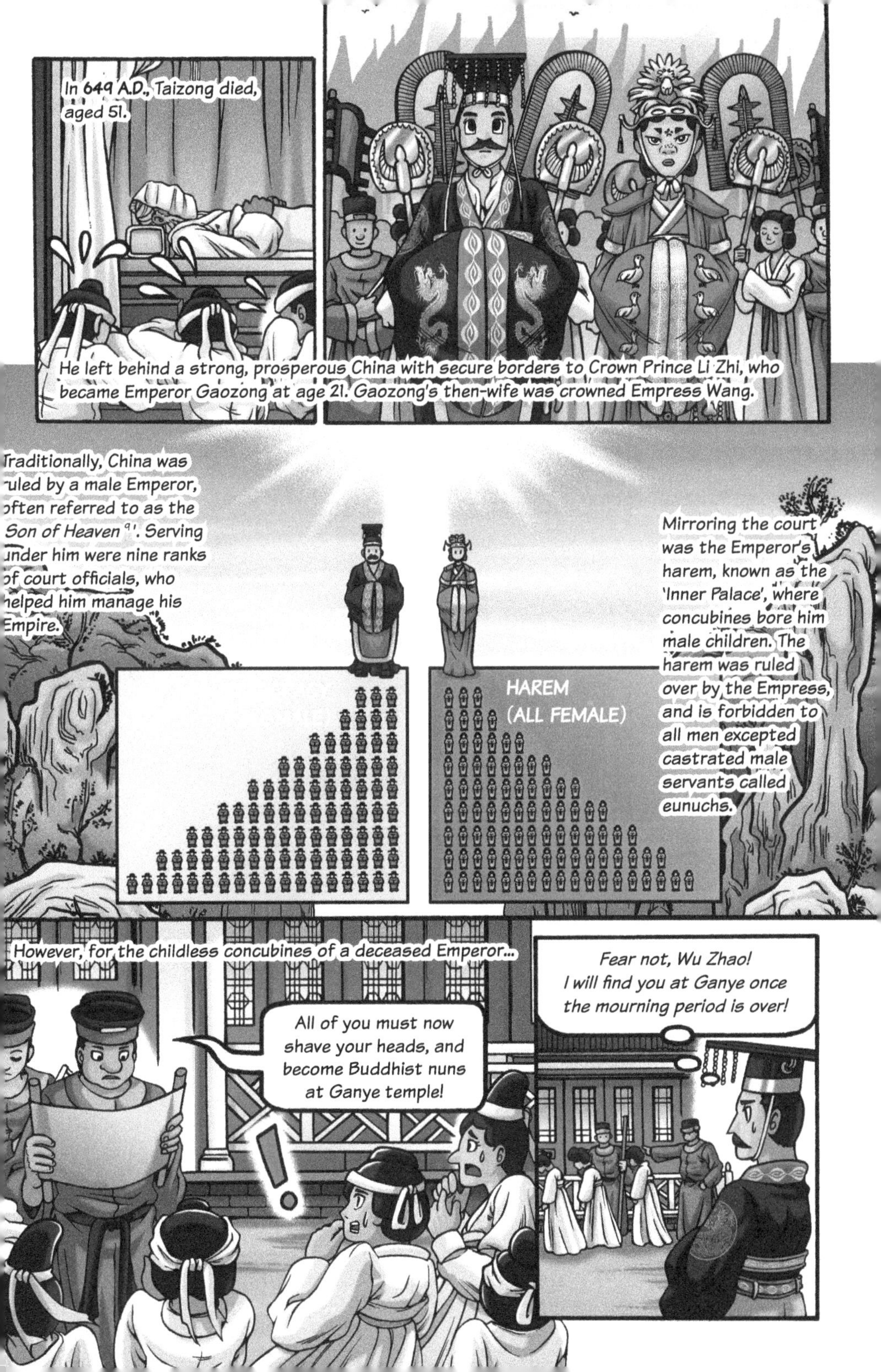
In 649 A.D., Taizong died, aged 51.
He left behind a strong, prosperous China with secure borders to Crown Prince Li Zhi, who became Emperor Gaozong at age 21. Gaozong's then-wife was crowned Empress Wang.
Traditionally, China was ruled by a male Emperor, often referred to as the 'Son of Heaven'[9]. Serving under him were nine ranks of court officials, who helped him manage his Empire.
HAREM (ALL FEMALE)
Mirroring the court was the Emperor's harem, known as the 'Inner Palace', where concubines bore him male children. The harem was ruled over by the Empress, and is forbidden to all men excepted castrated male servants called eunuchs.
However, for the childless concubines of a deceased Emperor...
All of you must now shave your heads, and become Buddhist nuns at Ganye temple!
Fear not, Wu Zhao! I will find you at Ganye once the mourning period is over!

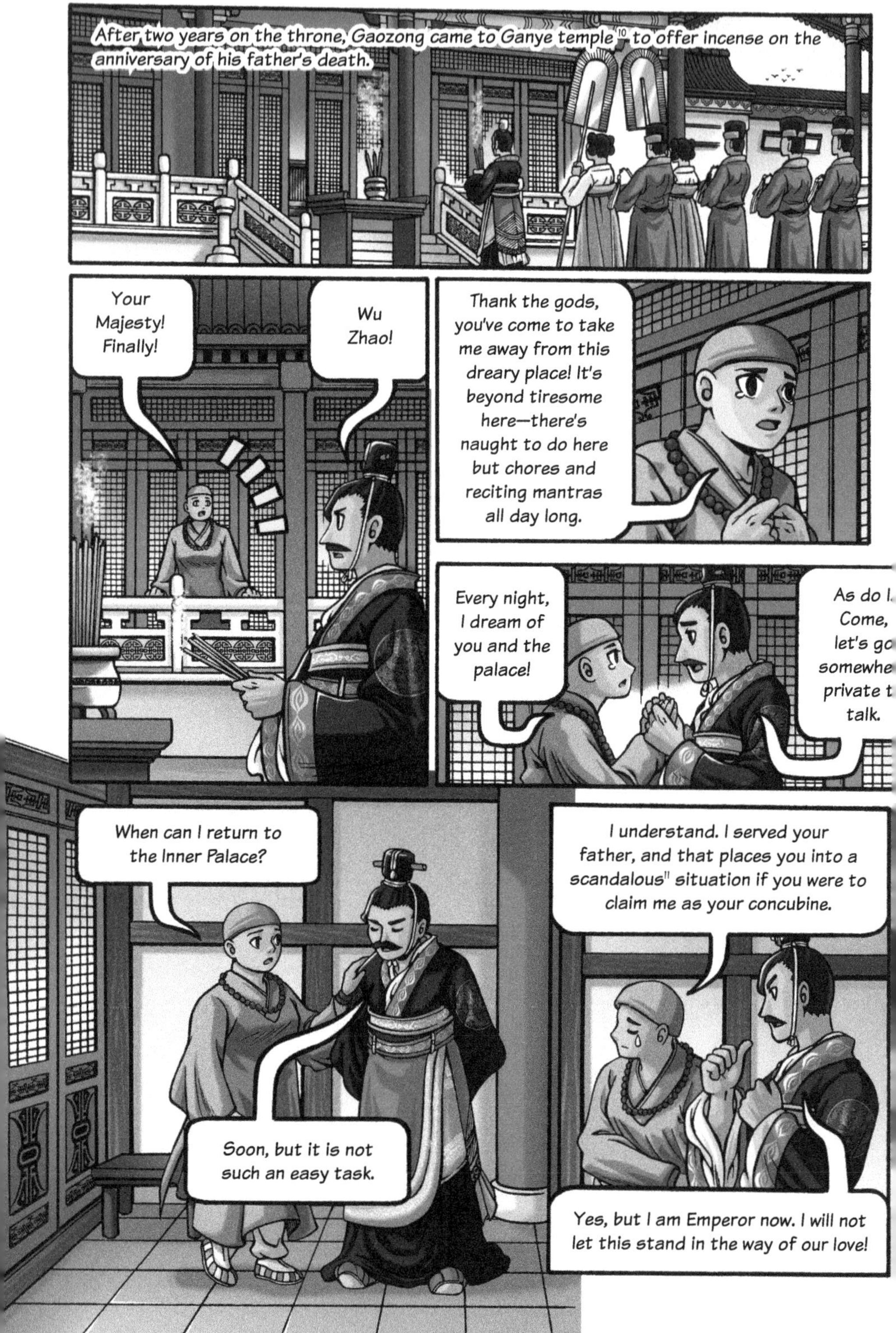
After two years on the throne, Gaozong came to Ganye temple[10] to offer incense on the anniversary of his father's death.
Your Majesty! Finally!
Wu Zhao!
Thank the gods, you've come to take me away from this dreary place! It's beyond tiresome here—there's naught to do here but chores and reciting mantras all day long.
Every night, I dream of you and the palace!
As do I. Come, let's go somewhe private t talk.
When can I return to the Inner Palace?
Soon, but it is not such an easy task.
I understand. I served your father, and that places you into a scandalous[11] situation if you were to claim me as your concubine.
Yes, but I am Emperor now. I will not let this stand in the way of our love!

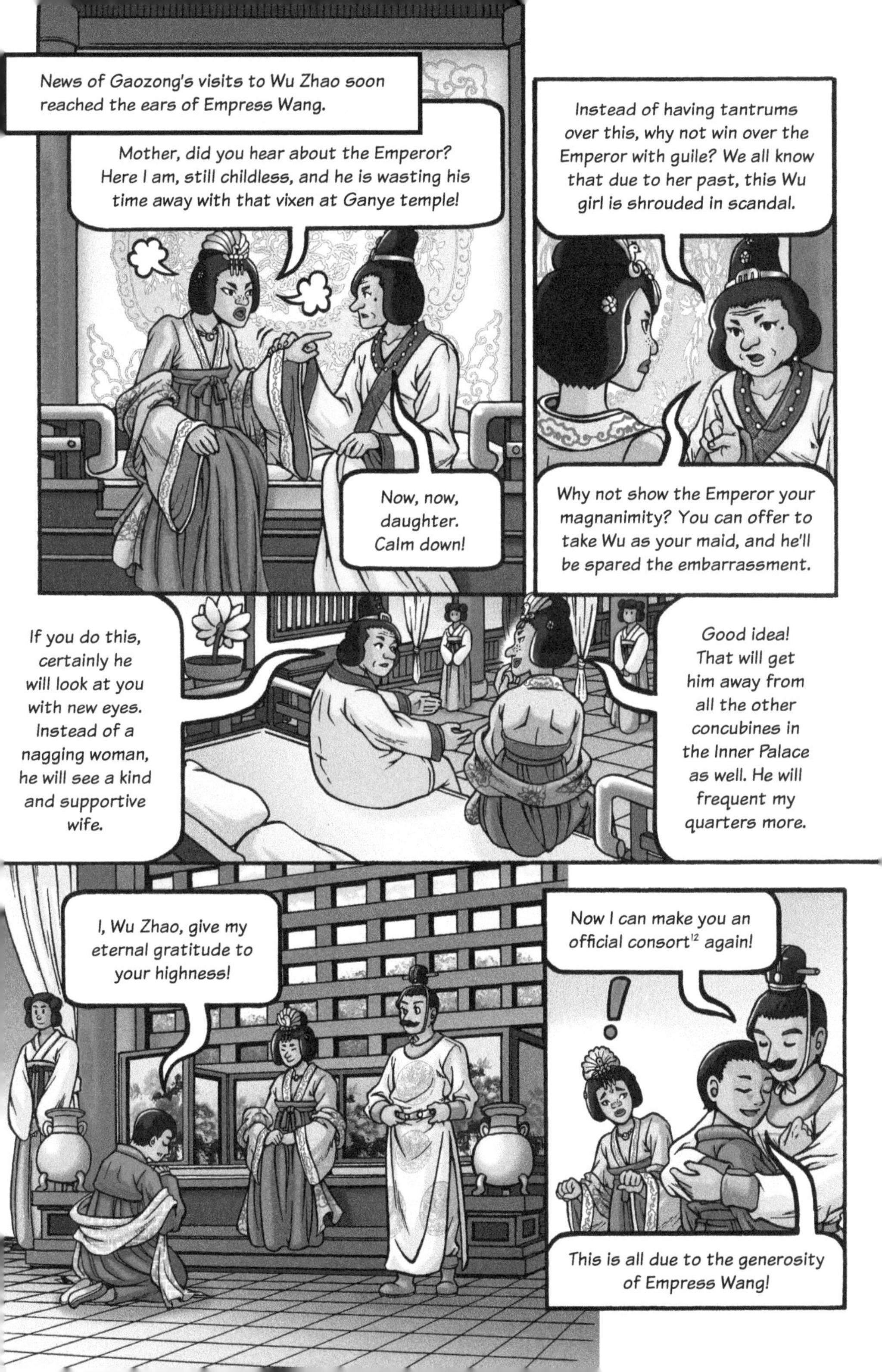
News of Gaozong's visits to Wu Zhao soon reached the ears of Empress Wang.
Mother, did you hear about the Emperor? Here I am, still childless, and he is wasting his time away with that vixen at Ganye temple!
Now, now, daughter. Calm down!
Instead of having tantrums over this, why not win over the Emperor with guile? We all know that due to her past, this Wu girl is shrouded in scandal.
Why not show the Emperor your magnanimity? You can offer to take Wu as your maid, and he'll be spared the embarrassment.
If you do this, certainly he will look at you with new eyes. Instead of a nagging woman, he will see a kind and supportive wife.
Good idea! That will get him away from all the other concubines in the Inner Palace as well. He will frequent my quarters more.
I, Wu Zhao, give my eternal gratitude to your highness!
Now I can make you an official consort[12] again!
!
This is all due to the generosity of Empress Wang!

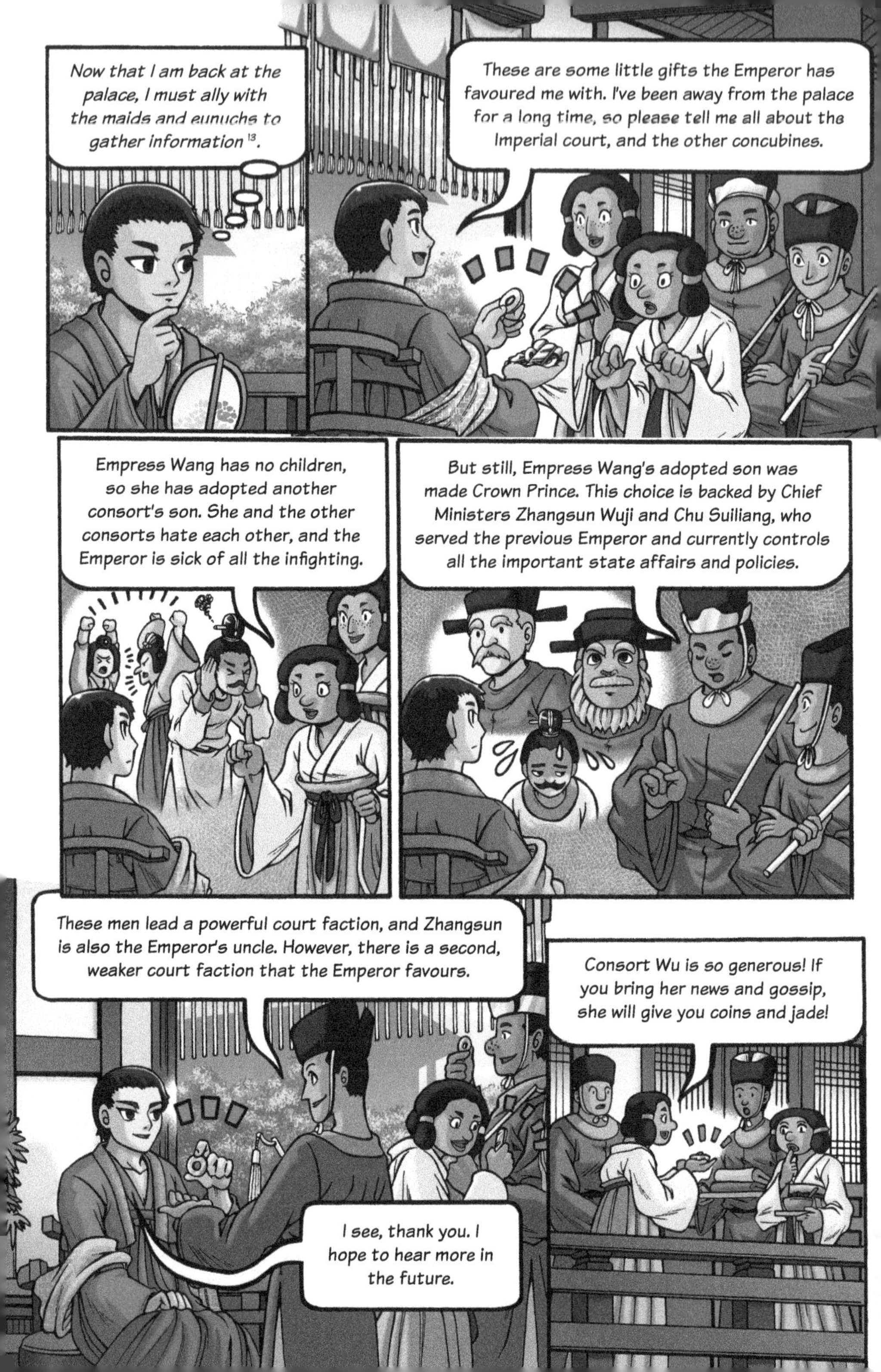
Now that I am back at the palace, I must ally with the maids and eunuchs to gather information[13].
These are some little gifts the Emperor has favoured me with. I've been away from the palace for a long time, so please tell me all about the Imperial court, and the other concubines.
Empress Wang has no children, so she has adopted another consort's son. She and the other consorts hate each other, and the Emperor is sick of all the infighting.
But still, Empress Wang's adopted son was made Crown Prince. This choice is backed by Chief Ministers Zhangsun Wuji and Chu Suiliang, who served the previous Emperor and currently controls all the important state affairs and policies.
These men lead a powerful court faction, and Zhangsun is also the Emperor's uncle. However, there is a second, weaker court faction that the Emperor favours.
I see, thank you. I hope to hear more in the future.
Consort Wu is so generous! If you bring her news and gossip, she will give you coins and jade!

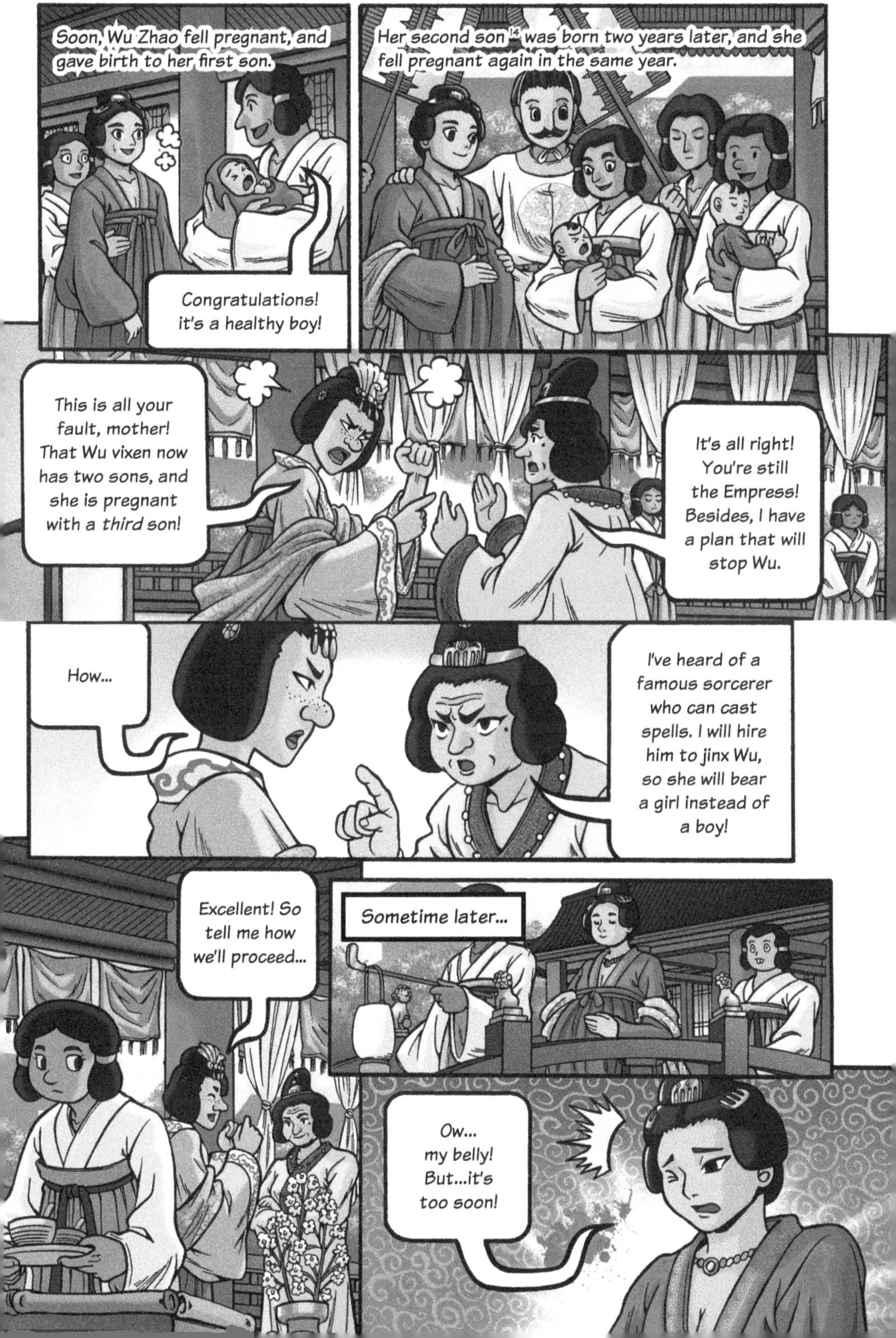
Soon, Wu Zhao fell pregnant, and gave birth to her first son.
Congratulations! it's a healthy boy!
Her second son[14] was born two years later, and she fell pregnant again in the same year.
This is all your fault, mother! That Wu vixen now has two sons, and she is pregnant with a *third* son!
It's all right! You're still the Empress! Besides, I have a plan that will stop Wu.
How...
I've heard of a famous sorcerer who can cast spells. I will hire him to jinx Wu, so she will bear a girl instead of a boy!
Excellent! So tell me how we'll proceed...
Sometime later...
Ow... my belly! But...it's too soon!

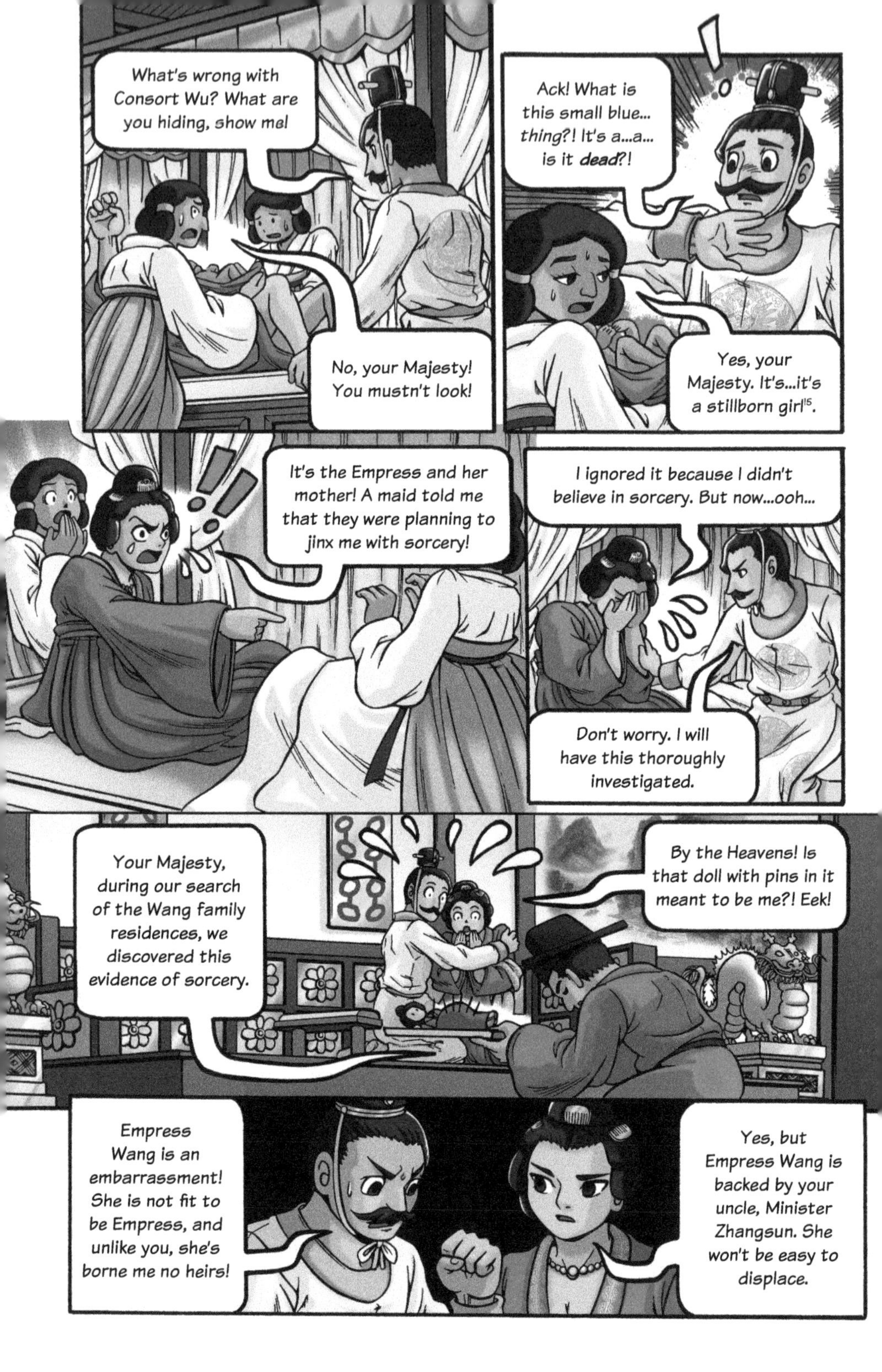
What's wrong with Consort Wu? What are you hiding, show me!
No, your Majesty! You mustn't look!
Ack! What is this small blue... *thing*?! It's a...a... is it *dead*?!
Yes, your Majesty. It's...it's a stillborn girl[15].
It's the Empress and her mother! A maid told me that they were planning to jinx me with sorcery!
I ignored it because I didn't believe in sorcery. But now...ooh...
Don't worry. I will have this thoroughly investigated.
Your Majesty, during our search of the Wang family residences, we discovered this evidence of sorcery.
By the Heavens! Is that doll with pins in it meant to be me?! Eek!
Empress Wang is an embarrassment! She is not fit to be Empress, and unlike you, she's borne me no heirs!
Yes, but Empress Wang is backed by your uncle, Minister Zhangsun. She won't be easy to displace.

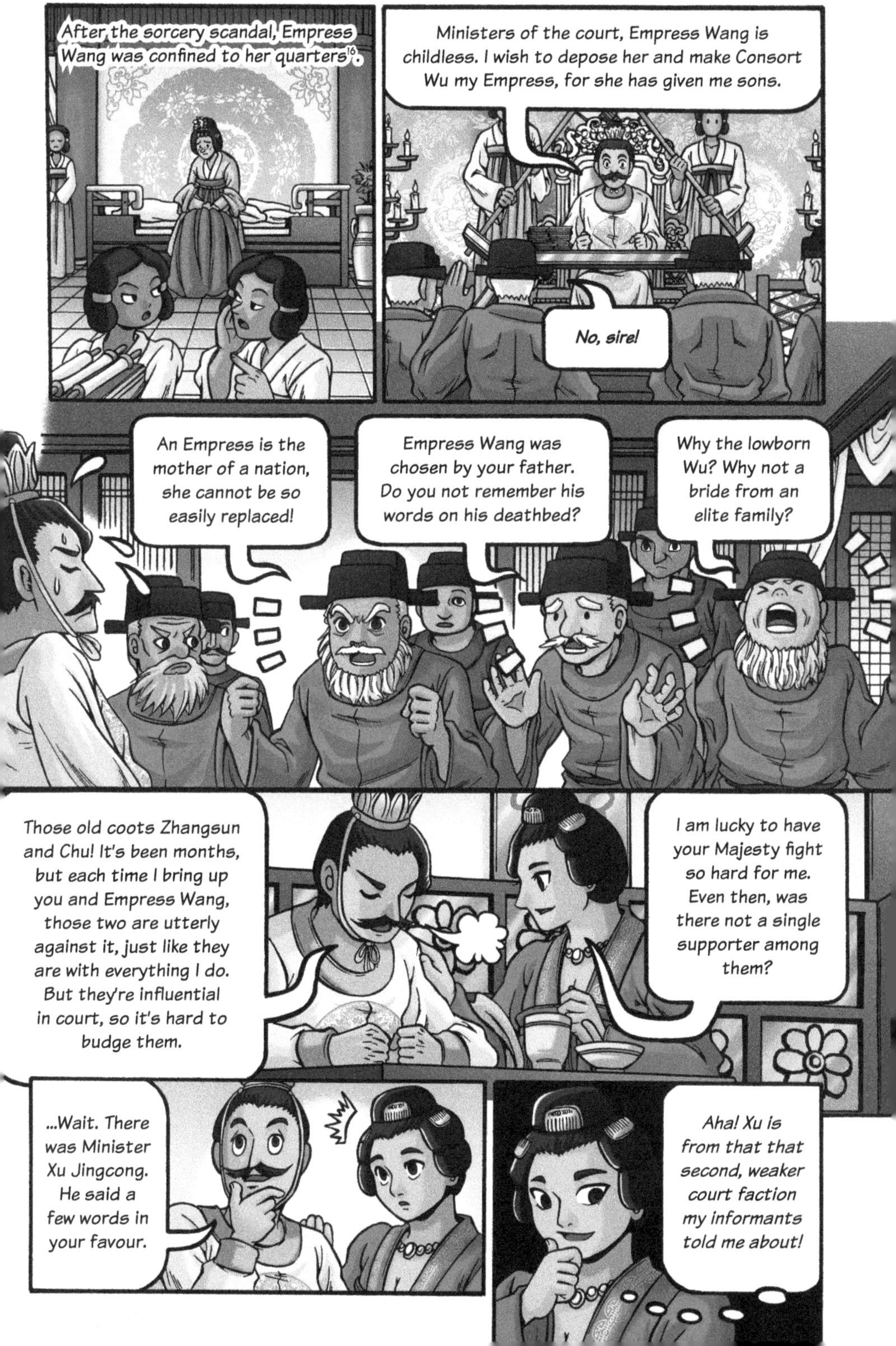
After the sorcery scandal, Empress Wang was confined to her quarters[16].
Ministers of the court, Empress Wang is childless. I wish to depose her and make Consort Wu my Empress, for she has given me sons.
No, sire!
An Empress is the mother of a nation, she cannot be so easily replaced!
Empress Wang was chosen by your father. Do you not remember his words on his deathbed?
Why the lowborn Wu? Why not a bride from an elite family?
Those old coots Zhangsun and Chu! It's been months, but each time I bring up you and Empress Wang, those two are utterly against it, just like they are with everything I do. But they're influential in court, so it's hard to budge them.
I am lucky to have your Majesty fight so hard for me. Even then, was there not a single supporter among them?
...Wait. There was Minister Xu Jingcong. He said a few words in your favour.
Aha! Xu is from that that second, weaker court faction my informants told me about!

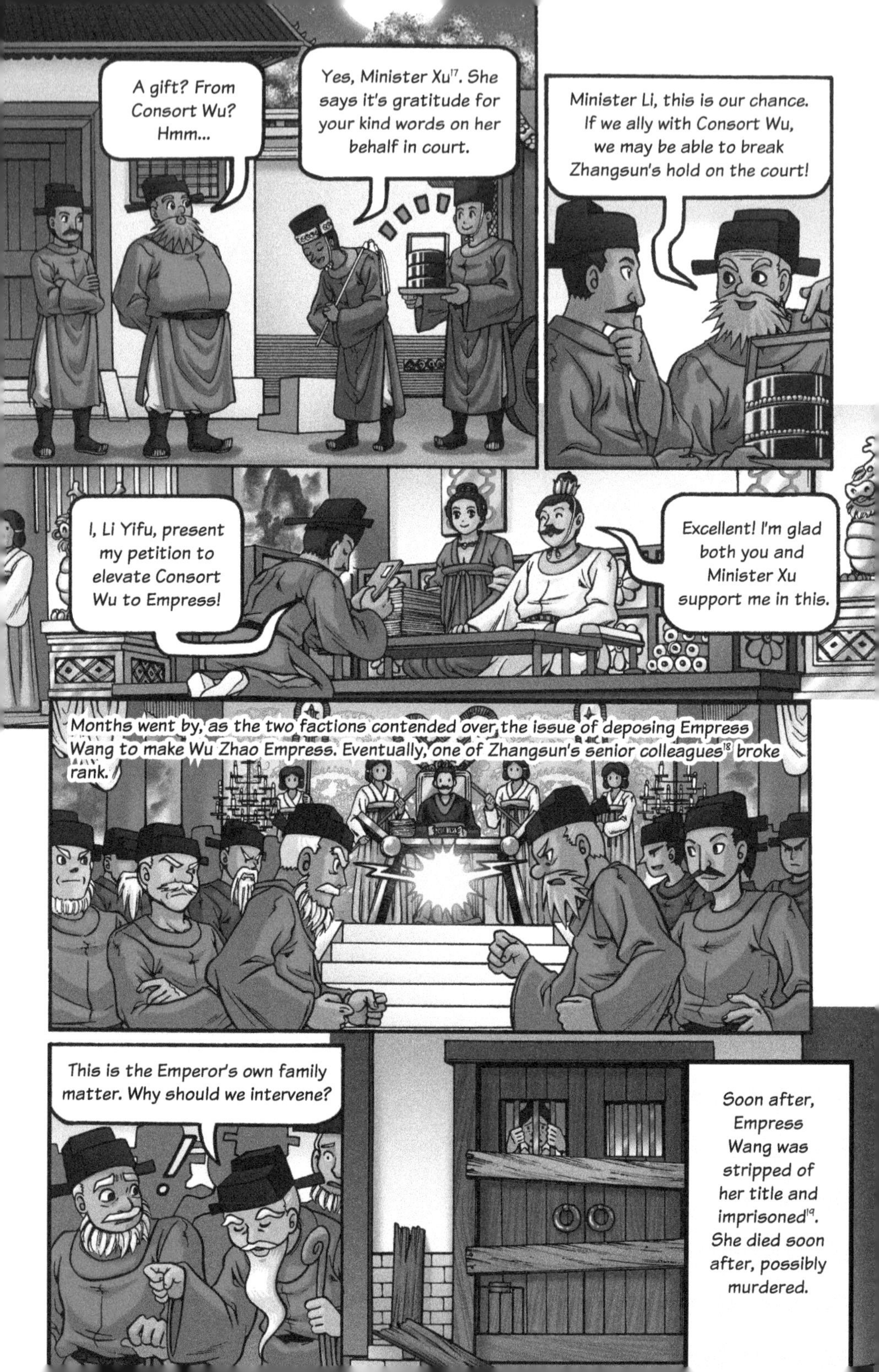
A gift? From Consort Wu? Hmm...
Yes, Minister Xu[17]. She says it's gratitude for your kind words on her behalf in court.
Minister Li, this is our chance. If we ally with Consort Wu, we may be able to break Zhangsun's hold on the court!
I, Li Yifu, present my petition to elevate Consort Wu to Empress!
Excellent! I'm glad both you and Minister Xu support me in this.
Months went by, as the two factions contended over the issue of deposing Empress Wang to make Wu Zhao Empress. Eventually, one of Zhangsun's senior colleagues[18] broke rank.
This is the Emperor's own family matter. Why should we intervene?
!?
Soon after, Empress Wang was stripped of her title and imprisoned[19]. She died soon after, possibly murdered.

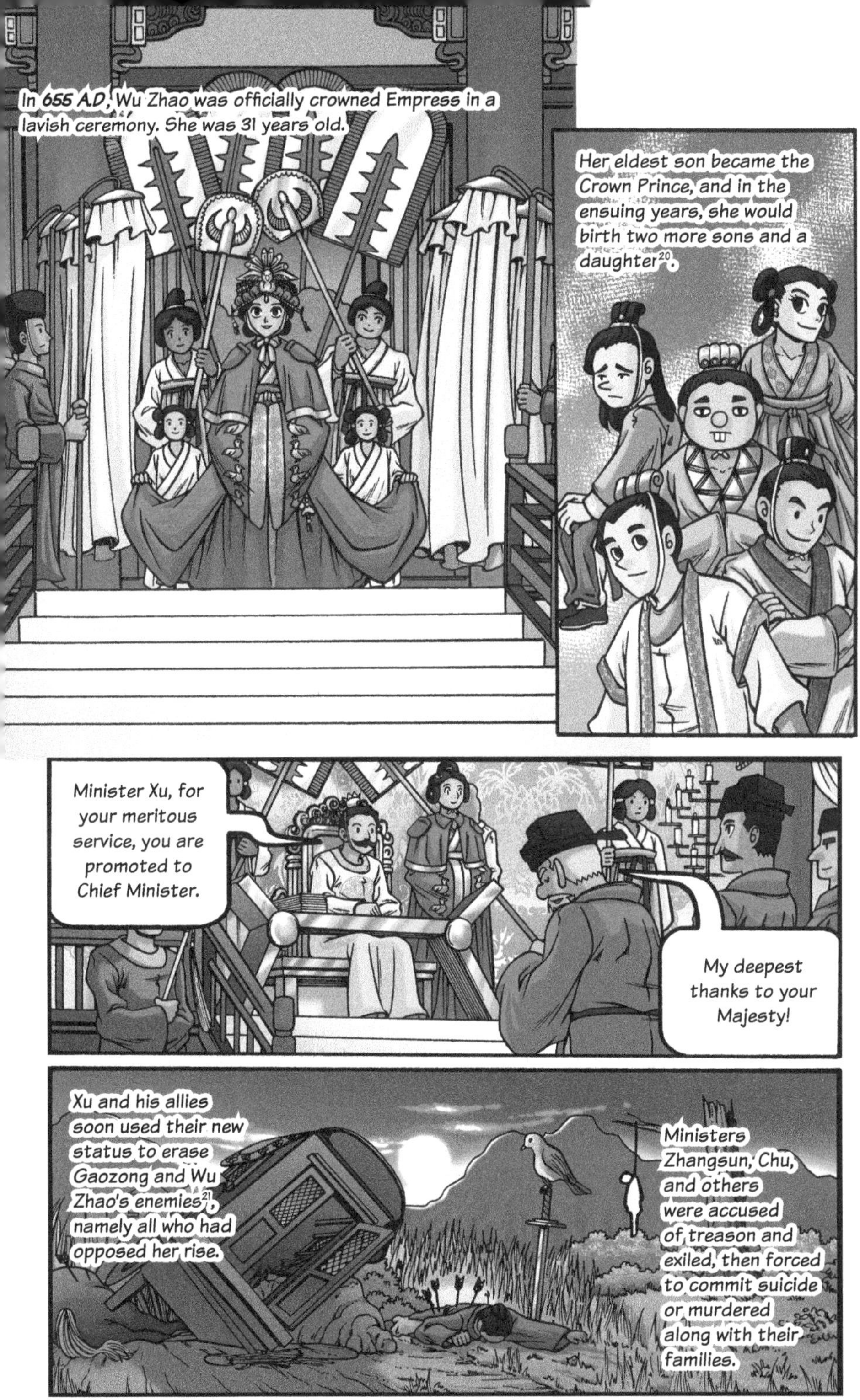
In 655 A.D, Wu Zhao was officially crowned Empress in a lavish ceremony. She was 31 years old.
Her eldest son became the Crown Prince, and in the ensuing years, she would birth two more sons and a daughter[20].
Minister Xu, for your meritous service, you are promoted to Chief Minister.
My deepest thanks to your Majesty!
Xu and his allies soon used their new status to erase Gaozong and Wu Zhao's enemies[21], namely all who had opposed her rise.
Ministers Zhangsun, Chu, and others were accused of treason and exiled, then forced to commit suicide or murdered along with their families.

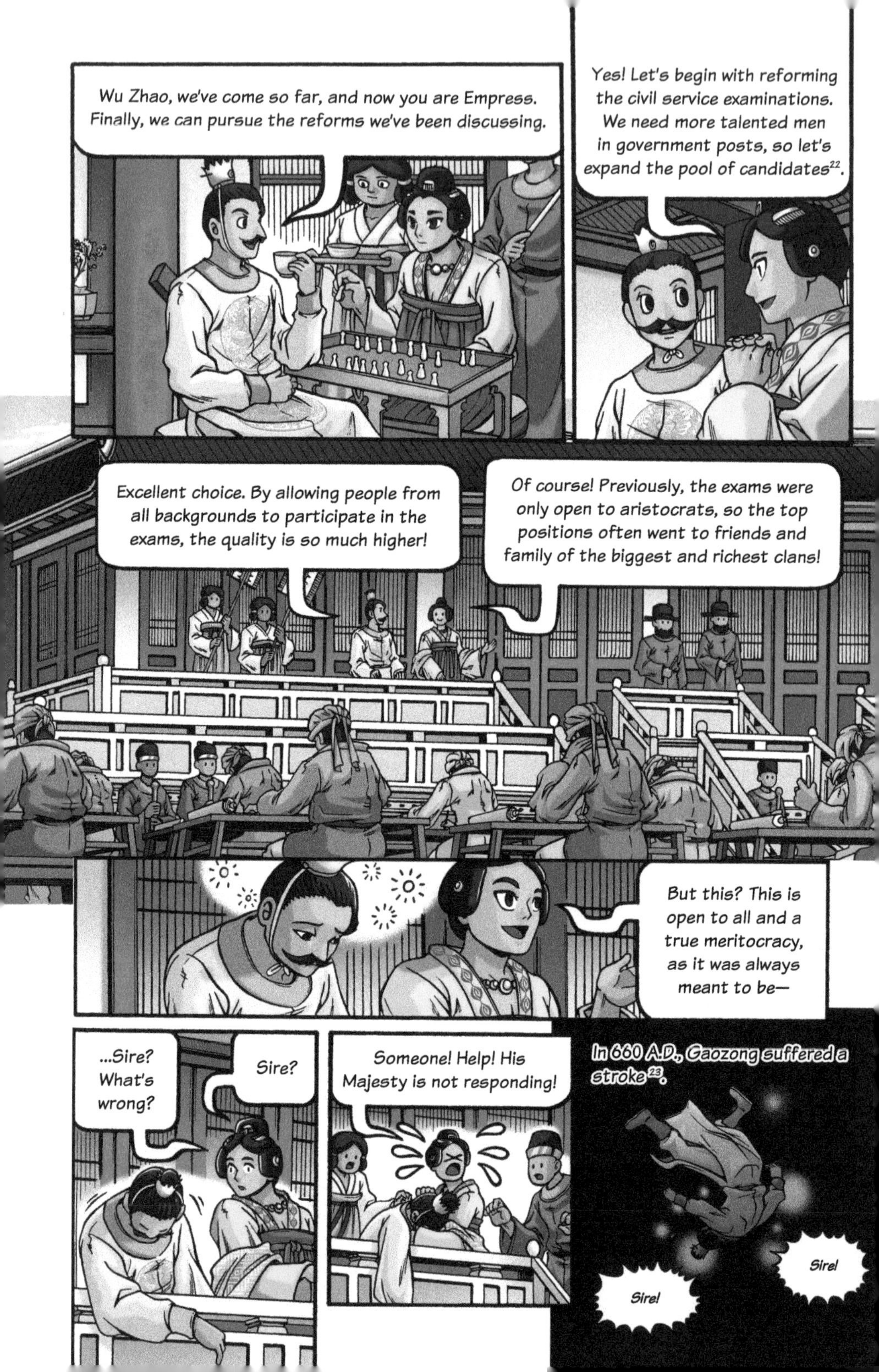
Wu Zhao, we've come so far, and now you are Empress. Finally, we can pursue the reforms we've been discussing.
Yes! Let's begin with reforming the civil service examinations. We need more talented men in government posts, so let's expand the pool of candidates[22].
Excellent choice. By allowing people from all backgrounds to participate in the exams, the quality is so much higher!
Of course! Previously, the exams were only open to aristocrats, so the top positions often went to friends and family of the biggest and richest clans!
But this? This is open to all and a true meritocracy, as it was always meant to be—
...Sire? What's wrong?
Sire?
Someone! Help! His Majesty is not responding!
In 660 A.D., Gaozong suffered a stroke[23].
Sire!
Sire!

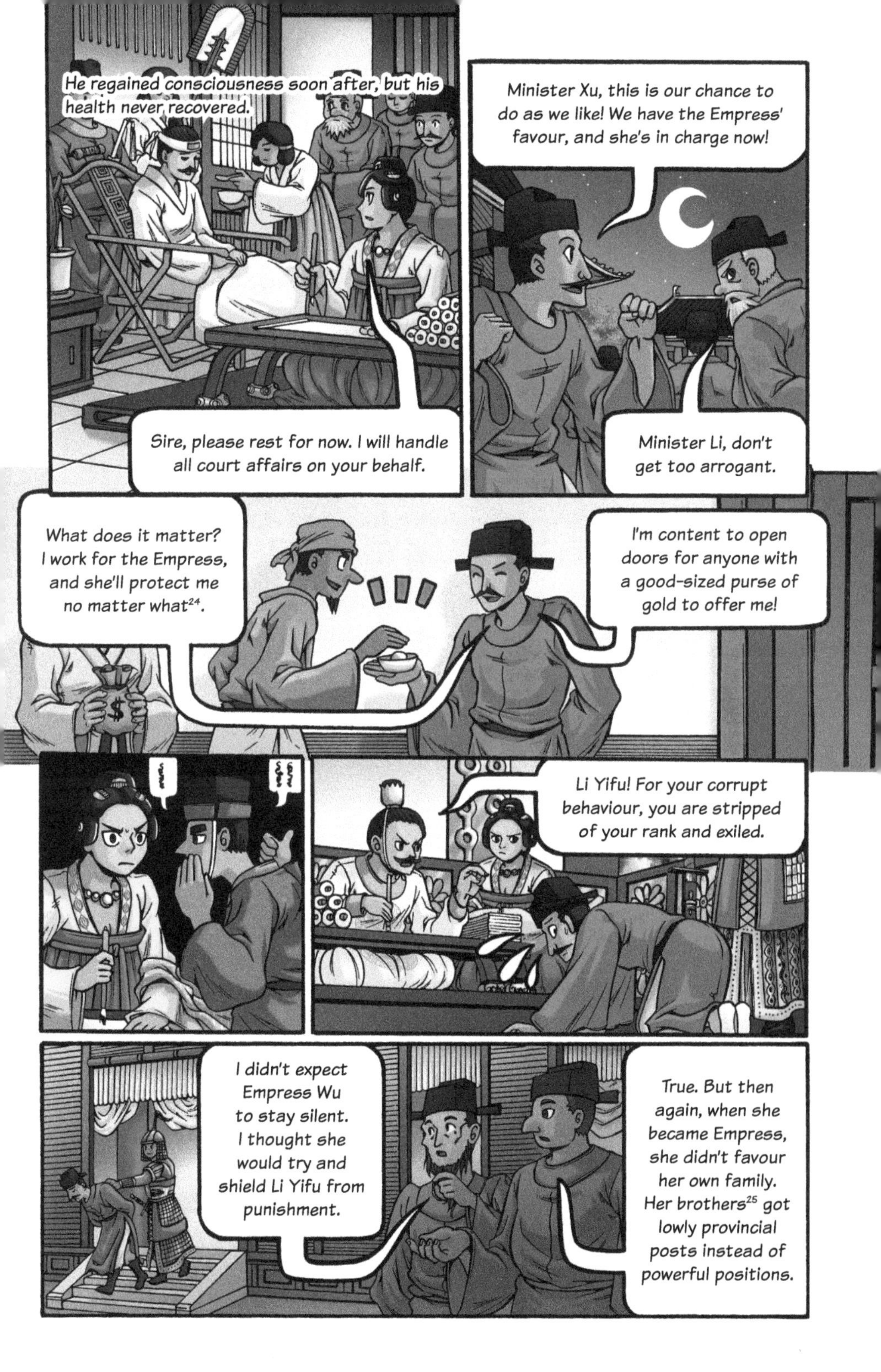
He regained consciousness soon after, but his health never recovered.
Sire, please rest for now. I will handle all court affairs on your behalf.
Minister Xu, this is our chance to do as we like! We have the Empress' favour, and she's in charge now!
Minister Li, don't get too arrogant.
What does it matter? I work for the Empress, and she'll protect me no matter what[24].
I'm content to open doors for anyone with a good-sized purse of gold to offer me!
Li Yifu! For your corrupt behaviour, you are stripped of your rank and exiled.
I didn't expect Empress Wu to stay silent. I thought she would try and shield Li Yifu from punishment.
True. But then again, when she became Empress, she didn't favour her own family. Her brothers[25] got lowly provincial posts instead of powerful positions.

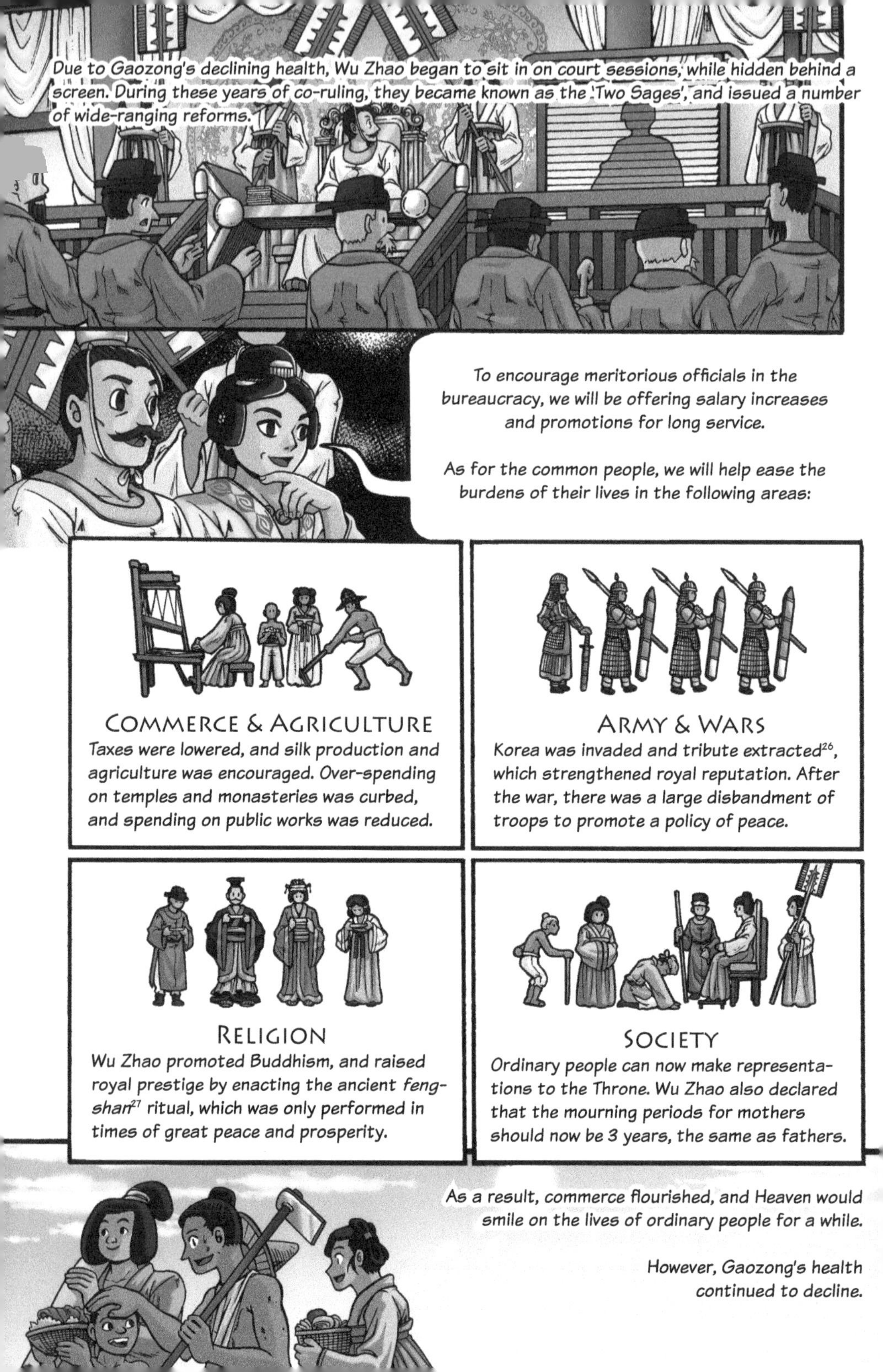
Due to Gaozong's declining health, Wu Zhao began to sit in on court sessions, while hidden behind a screen. During these years of co-ruling, they became known as the 'Two Sages', and issued a number of wide-ranging reforms.
To encourage meritorious officials in the bureaucracy, we will be offering salary increases and promotions for long service.
As for the common people, we will help ease the burdens of their lives in the following areas:
COMMERCE & AGRICULTURE
Taxes were lowered, and silk production and agriculture was encouraged. Over-spending on temples and monasteries was curbed, and spending on public works was reduced.
ARMY & WARS
Korea was invaded and tribute extracted[26], which strengthened royal reputation. After the war, there was a large disbandment of troops to promote a policy of peace.
RELIGION
Wu Zhao promoted Buddhism, and raised royal prestige by enacting the ancient *feng-shan*[27] ritual, which was only performed in times of great peace and prosperity.
SOCIETY
Ordinary people can now make representations to the Throne. Wu Zhao also declared that the mourning periods for mothers should now be 3 years, the same as fathers.
As a result, commerce flourished, and Heaven would smile on the lives of ordinary people for a while.
However, Gaozong's health continued to decline.

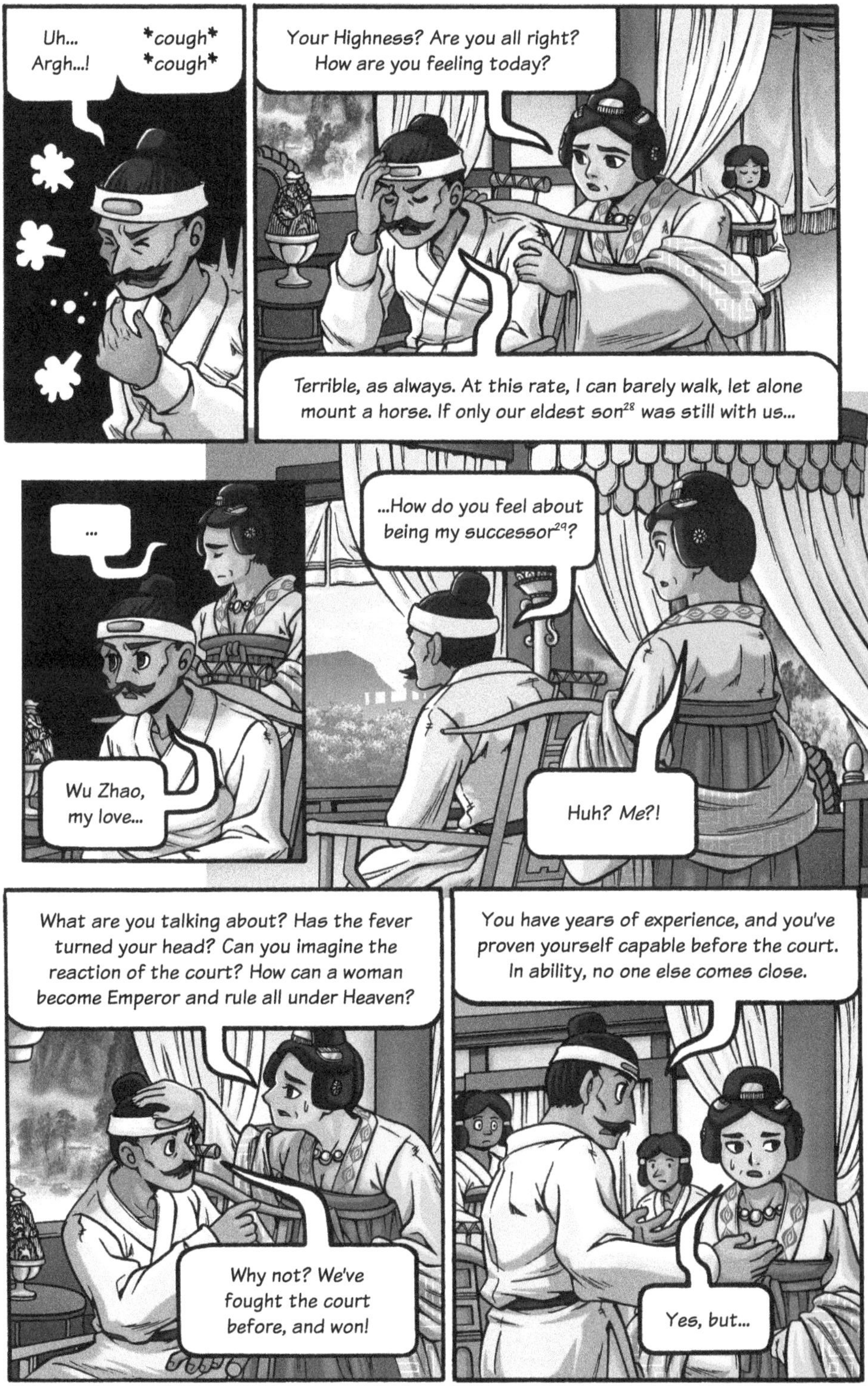

Uh... Argh...!
cough *cough*
Your Highness? Are you all right? How are you feeling today?
Terrible, as always. At this rate, I can barely walk, let alone mount a horse. If only our eldest son[28] was still with us...
...
Wu Zhao, my love...
...How do you feel about being my successor[29]?
Huh? Me?!
What are you talking about? Has the fever turned your head? Can you imagine the reaction of the court? How can a woman become Emperor and rule all under Heaven?
Why not? We've fought the court before, and won!
You have years of experience, and you've proven yourself capable before the court. In ability, no one else comes close.
Yes, but...

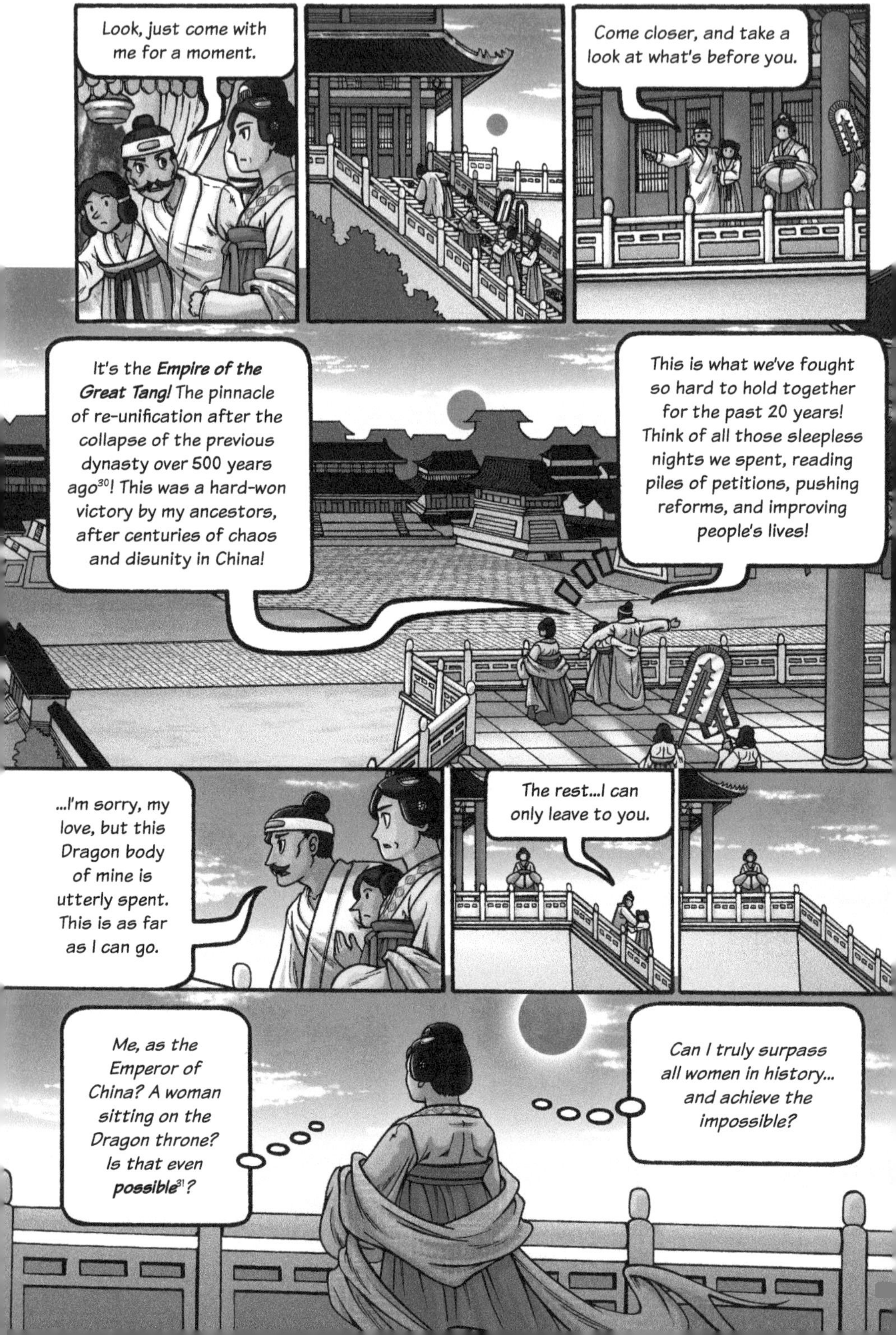
Look, just come with me for a moment.
Come closer, and take a look at what's before you.
It's the Empire of the Great Tang! The pinnacle of re-unification after the collapse of the previous dynasty over 500 years ago[30]! This was a hard-won victory by my ancestors, after centuries of chaos and disunity in China!
This is what we've fought so hard to hold together for the past 20 years! Think of all those sleepless nights we spent, reading piles of petitions, pushing reforms, and improving people's lives!
...I'm sorry, my love, but this Dragon body of mine is utterly spent. This is as far as I can go.
The rest...I can only leave to you.
Me, as the Emperor of China? A woman sitting on the Dragon throne? Is that even possible[31]?
Can I truly surpass all women in history... and achieve the impossible?

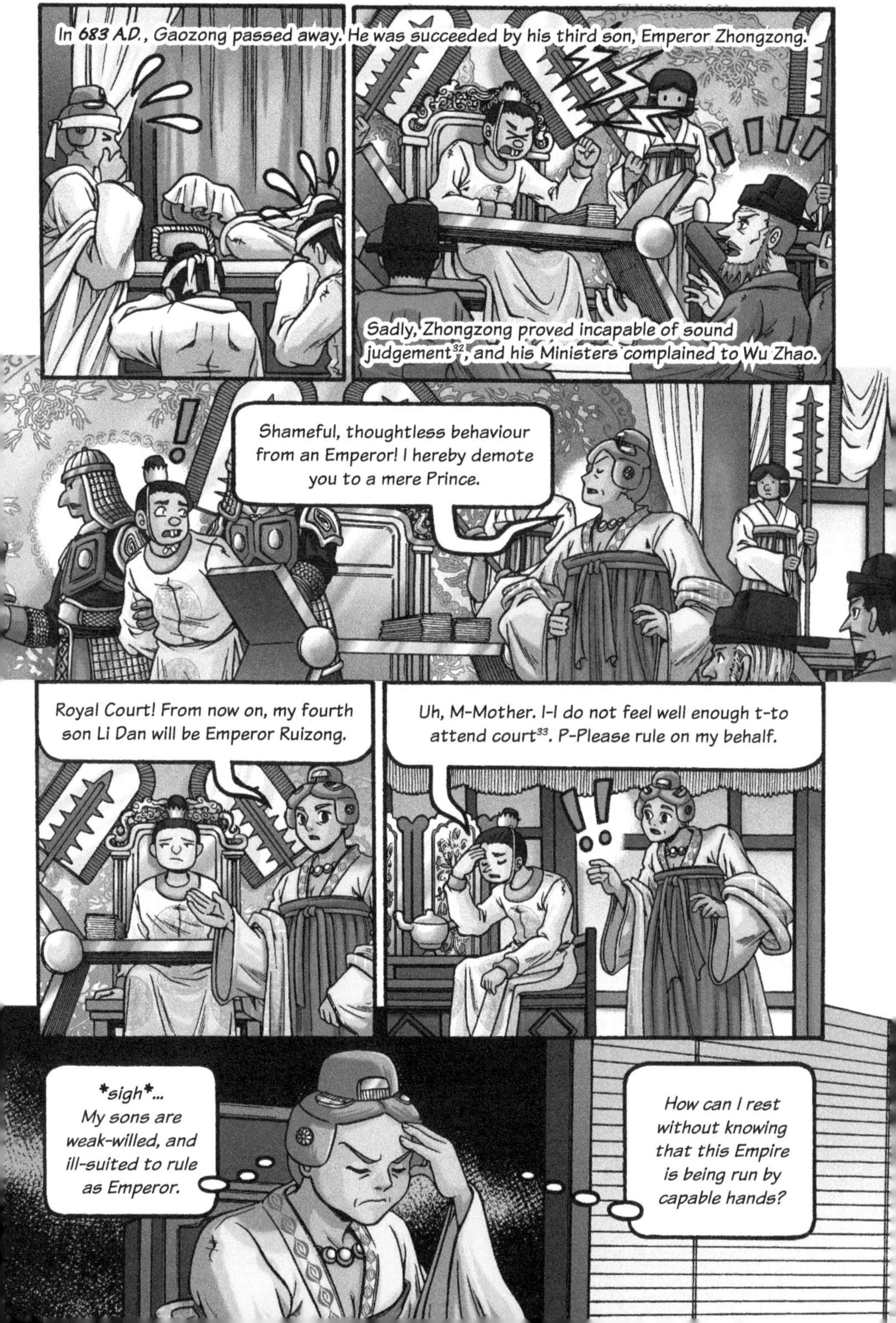

In 683 A.D., Gaozong passed away. He was succeeded by his third son, Emperor Zhongzong.
Sadly, Zhongzong proved incapable of sound judgement[32], and his Ministers complained to Wu Zhao.
Shameful, thoughtless behaviour from an Emperor! I hereby demote you to a mere Prince.
Royal Court! From now on, my fourth son Li Dan will be Emperor Ruizong.
Uh, M-Mother. I-I do not feel well enough t-to attend court[33]. P-Please rule on my behalf.
sigh... My sons are weak-willed, and ill-suited to rule as Emperor.
How can I rest without knowing that this Empire is being run by capable hands?

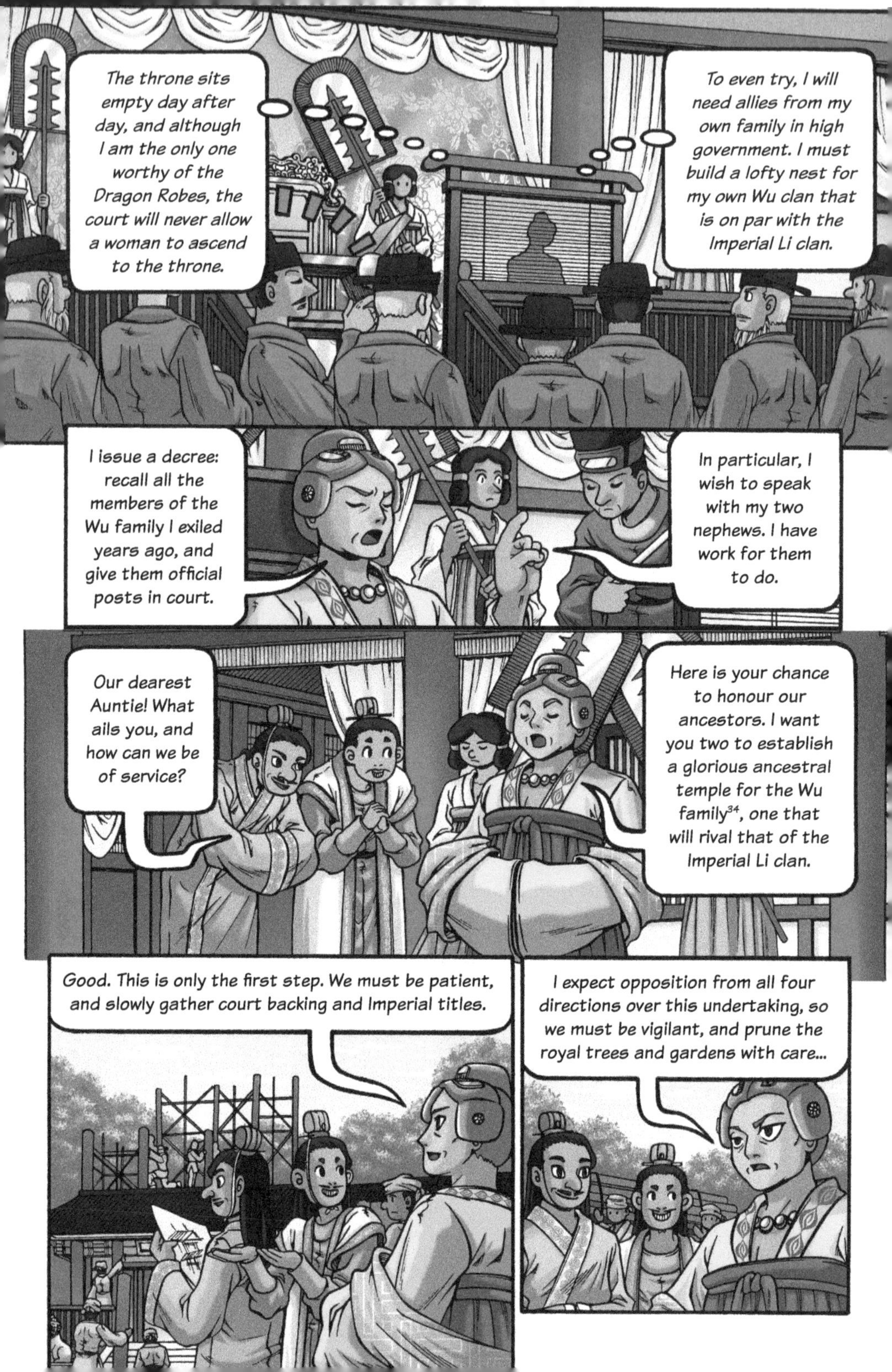
The throne sits empty day after day, and although I am the only one worthy of the Dragon Robes, the court will never allow a woman to ascend to the throne.
To even try, I will need allies from my own family in high government. I must build a lofty nest for my own Wu clan that is on par with the Imperial Li clan.
I issue a decree: recall all the members of the Wu family I exiled years ago, and give them official posts in court.
In particular, I wish to speak with my two nephews. I have work for them to do.
Our dearest Auntie! What ails you, and how can we be of service?
Here is your chance to honour our ancestors. I want you two to establish a glorious ancestral temple for the Wu family[34], one that will rival that of the Imperial Li clan.
Good. This is only the first step. We must be patient, and slowly gather court backing and Imperial titles.
I expect opposition from all four directions over this undertaking, so we must be vigilant, and prune the royal trees and gardens with care...

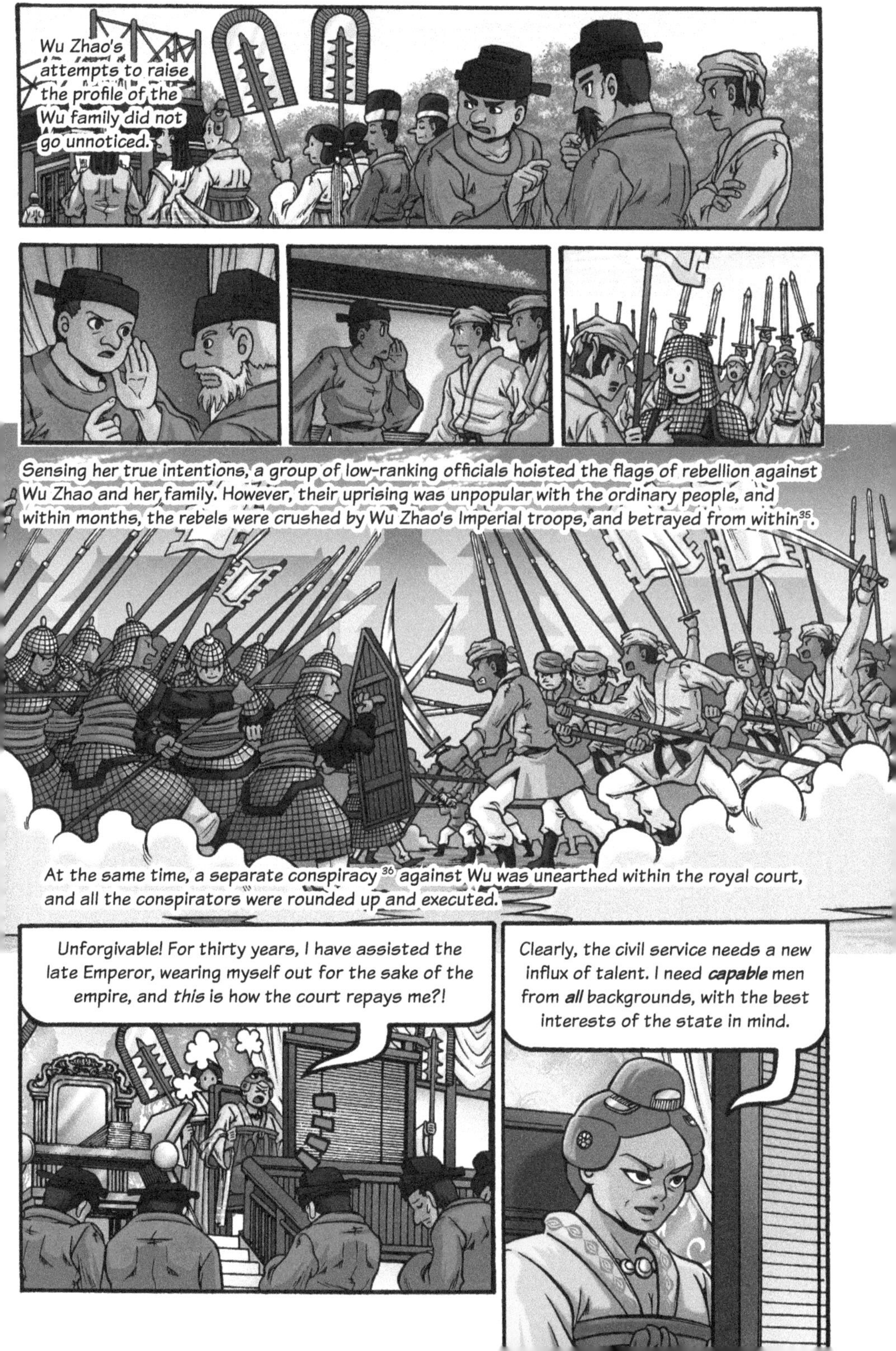
Wu Zhao's attempts to raise the profile of the Wu family did not go unnoticed.
Sensing her true intentions, a group of low-ranking officials hoisted the flags of rebellion against Wu Zhao and her family. However, their uprising was unpopular with the ordinary people, and within months, the rebels were crushed by Wu Zhao's Imperial troops, and betrayed from within[35].
At the same time, a separate conspiracy[36] against Wu was unearthed within the royal court, and all the conspirators were rounded up and executed.
Unforgivable! For thirty years, I have assisted the late Emperor, wearing myself out for the sake of the empire, and *this* is how the court repays me?!
Clearly, the civil service needs a new influx of talent. I need ***capable*** men from ***all*** backgrounds, with the best interests of the state in mind.

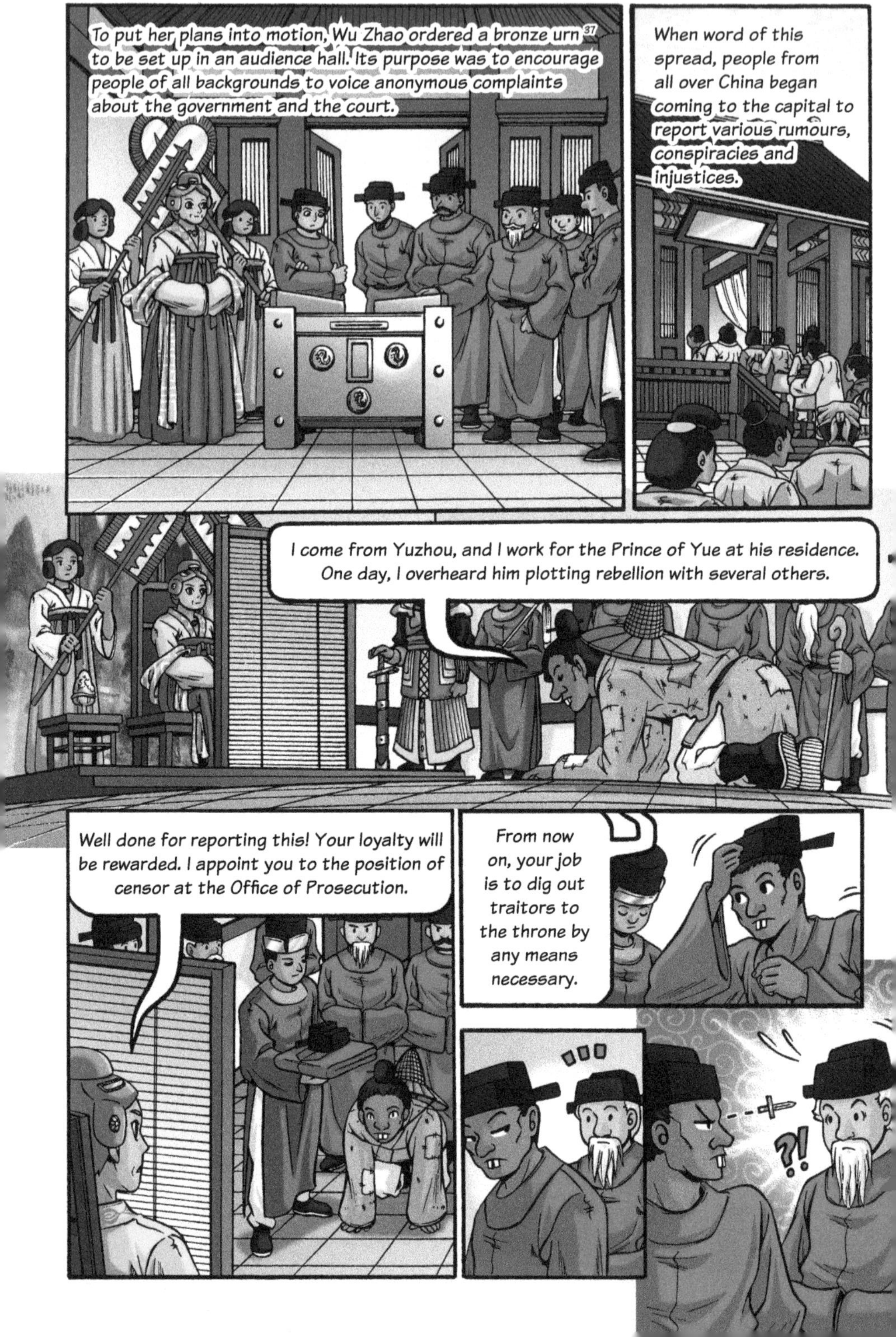
To put her plans into motion, Wu Zhao ordered a bronze urn[37] to be set up in an audience hall. Its purpose was to encourage people of all backgrounds to voice anonymous complaints about the government and the court.
When word of this spread, people from all over China began coming to the capital to report various rumours, conspiracies and injustices.
I come from Yuzhou, and I work for the Prince of Yue at his residence. One day, I overheard him plotting rebellion with several others.
Well done for reporting this! Your loyalty will be rewarded. I appoint you to the position of censor at the Office of Prosecution.
From now on, your job is to dig out traitors to the throne by any means necessary.
?!

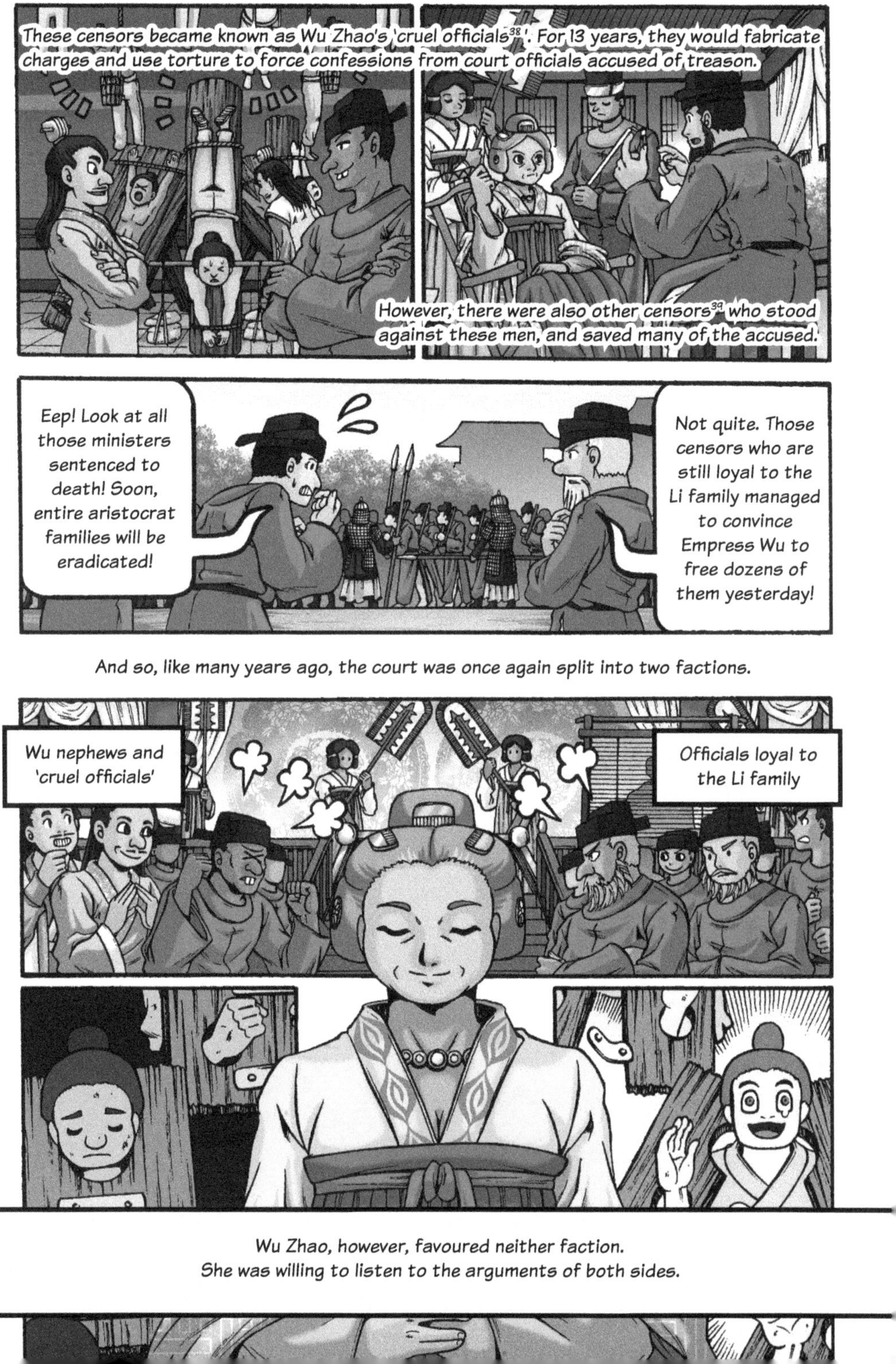
These censors became known as Wu Zhao's 'cruel officials[38]'. For 13 years, they would fabricate charges and use torture to force confessions from court officials accused of treason.
However, there were also other censors[39] who stood against these men, and saved many of the accused.
Eep! Look at all those ministers sentenced to death! Soon, entire aristocrat families will be eradicated!
Not quite. Those censors who are still loyal to the Li family managed to convince Empress Wu to free dozens of them yesterday!
And so, like many years ago, the court was once again split into two factions.
Wu nephews and 'cruel officials'
Officials loyal to the Li family
Wu Zhao, however, favoured neither faction.
She was willing to listen to the arguments of both sides.

Over the next few years, Wu Zhao slowly gathered all the titles required for an Emperor.

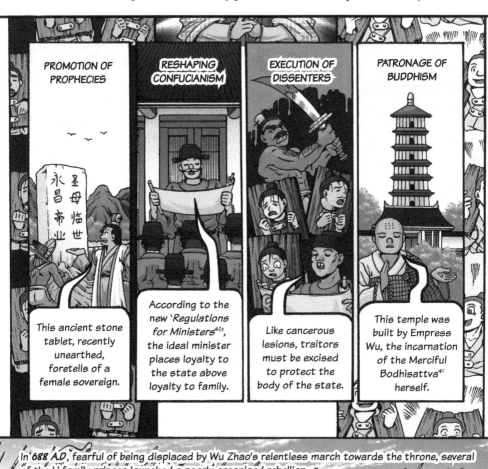

PROMOTION OF PROPHECIES

This ancient stone tablet, recently unearthed, foretells of a female sovereign.

RESHAPING CONFUCIANISM

According to the new 'Regulations for Ministers[40]', the ideal minister places loyalty to the state above loyalty to family.

EXECUTION OF DISSENTERS

Like cancerous lesions, traitors must be excised to protect the body of the state.

PATRONAGE OF BUDDHISM

This temple was built by Empress Wu, the incarnation of the Merciful Bodhisattva[41] herself.

In 688 AD, fearful of being displaced by Wu Zhao's relentless march towards the throne, several of the Li family princes launched a poorly organised rebellion.

It was even less popular than the first rebellion from four years ago, and was crushed within a week[42].

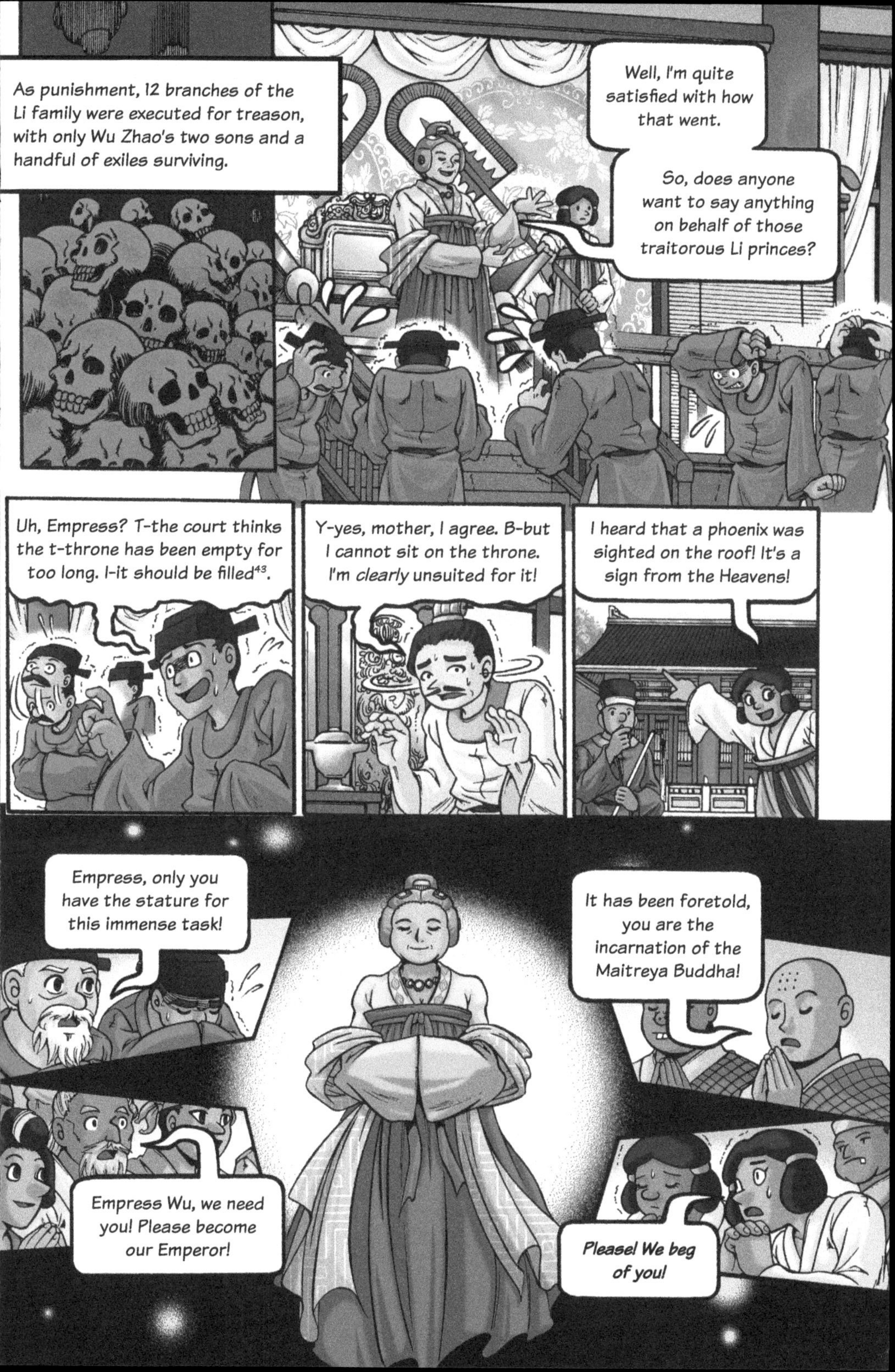
As punishment, 12 branches of the Li family were executed for treason, with only Wu Zhao's two sons and a handful of exiles surviving.
Well, I'm quite satisfied with how that went.
So, does anyone want to say anything on behalf of those traitorous Li princes?
Uh, Empress? T-the court thinks the t-throne has been empty for too long. I-it should be filled[43].
Y-yes, mother, I agree. B-but I cannot sit on the throne. I'm *clearly* unsuited for it!
I heard that a phoenix was sighted on the roof! It's a sign from the Heavens!
Empress, only you have the stature for this immense task!
It has been foretold, you are the incarnation of the Maitreya Buddha!
Empress Wu, we need you! Please become our Emperor!
Please! We beg of you!

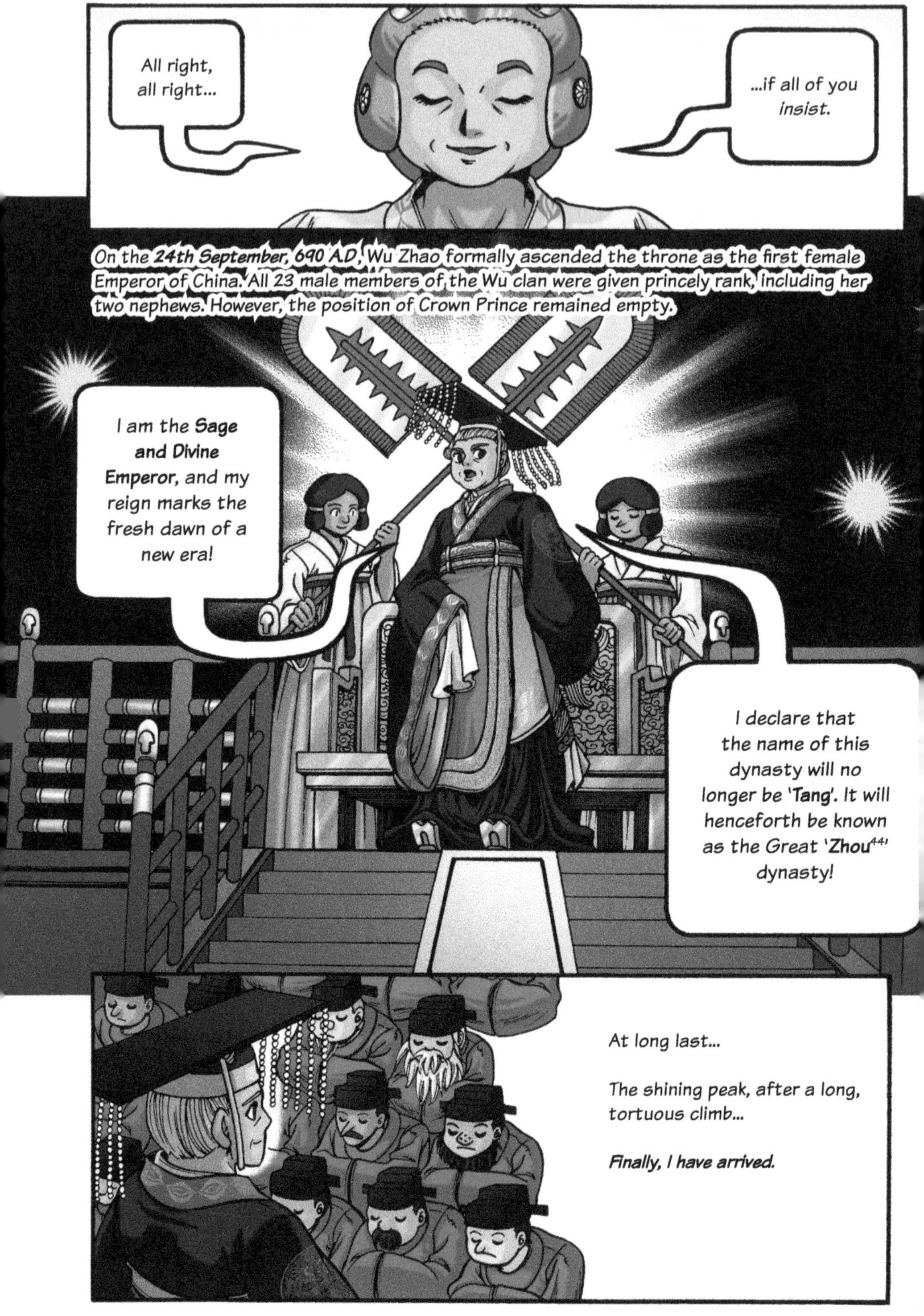
All right, all right...
...if all of you *insist.*
On the ***24th September, 690 A.D***, Wu Zhao formally ascended the throne as the first female Emperor of China. All 23 male members of the Wu clan were given princely rank, including her two nephews. However, the position of Crown Prince remained empty.
I am the **Sage and Divine Emperor**, and my reign marks the fresh dawn of a new era!
I declare that the name of this dynasty will no longer be '**Tang**'. It will henceforth be known as the Great '**Zhou**[44]' dynasty!
At long last...
The shining peak, after a long, tortuous climb...
Finally, I have arrived.

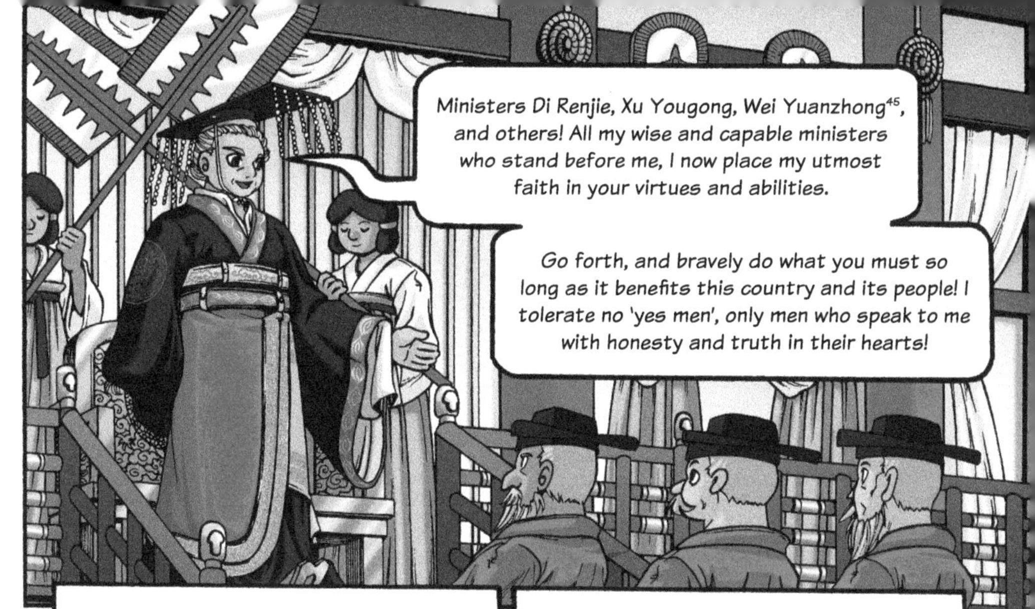
Ministers Di Renjie, Xu Yougong, Wei Yuanzhong[45], and others! All my wise and capable ministers who stand before me, I now place my utmost faith in your virtues and abilities.
Go forth, and bravely do what you must so long as it benefits this country and its people! I tolerate no 'yes men', only men who speak to me with honesty and truth in their hearts!

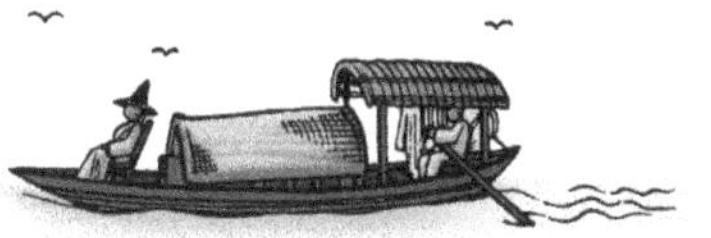

Commerce & Agriculture

The capital was moved to Luoyang[46], where its waterways encouraged trade and new settlers. Granaries were established in case of famine, the Silk Road was secured, and soldiers were fed by state-owned farms.

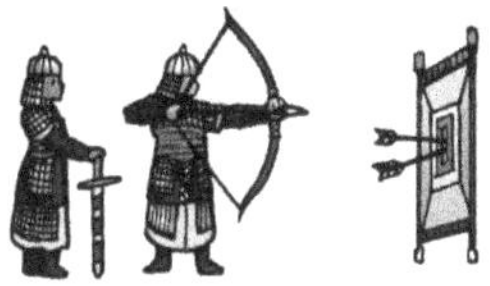

Army & Wars

Wu Zhao created a military exam[47] to find and test for competent generals. Three major foreign threats to China's borders, the Tibetans, Khitans, and Turks, were also defeated through diplomacy and war[48].

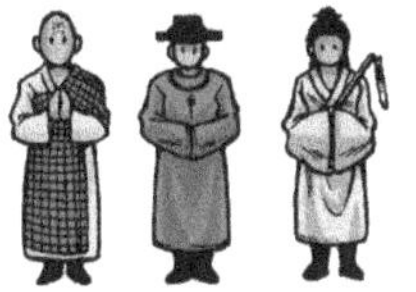

Religion

The fengshan[49] ritual was held a second time, and Wu Zhao continued to patronise Buddhist culture and art. Buddhism was officially raised to the status of a state religion[50], equal to Confucianism and Taoism.

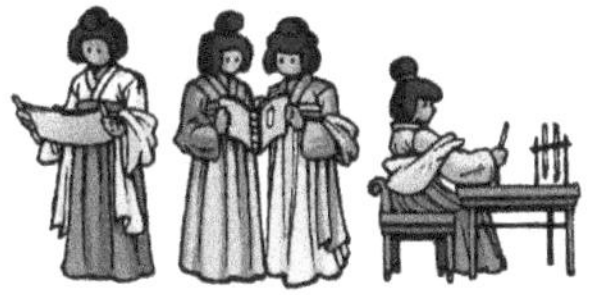

Society

Wu Zhao began personally testing the candidates for the civil service examinations. She also required all palace women to be educated, and chose the best essayist to be her secretary[51].

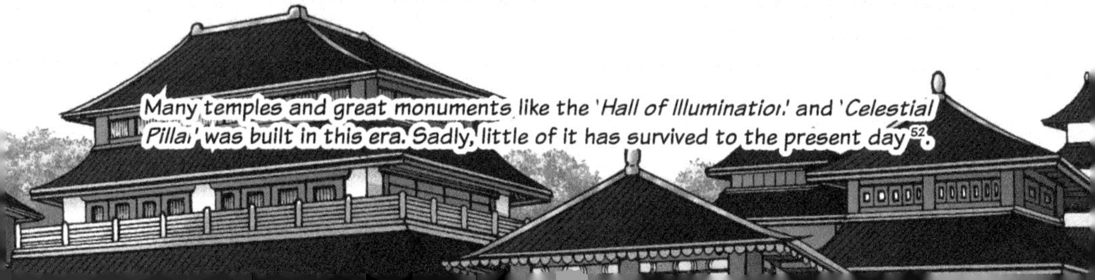
Many temples and great monuments like the 'Hall of Illumination' and 'Celestial Pillar' was built in this era. Sadly, little of it has survived to the present day[52].

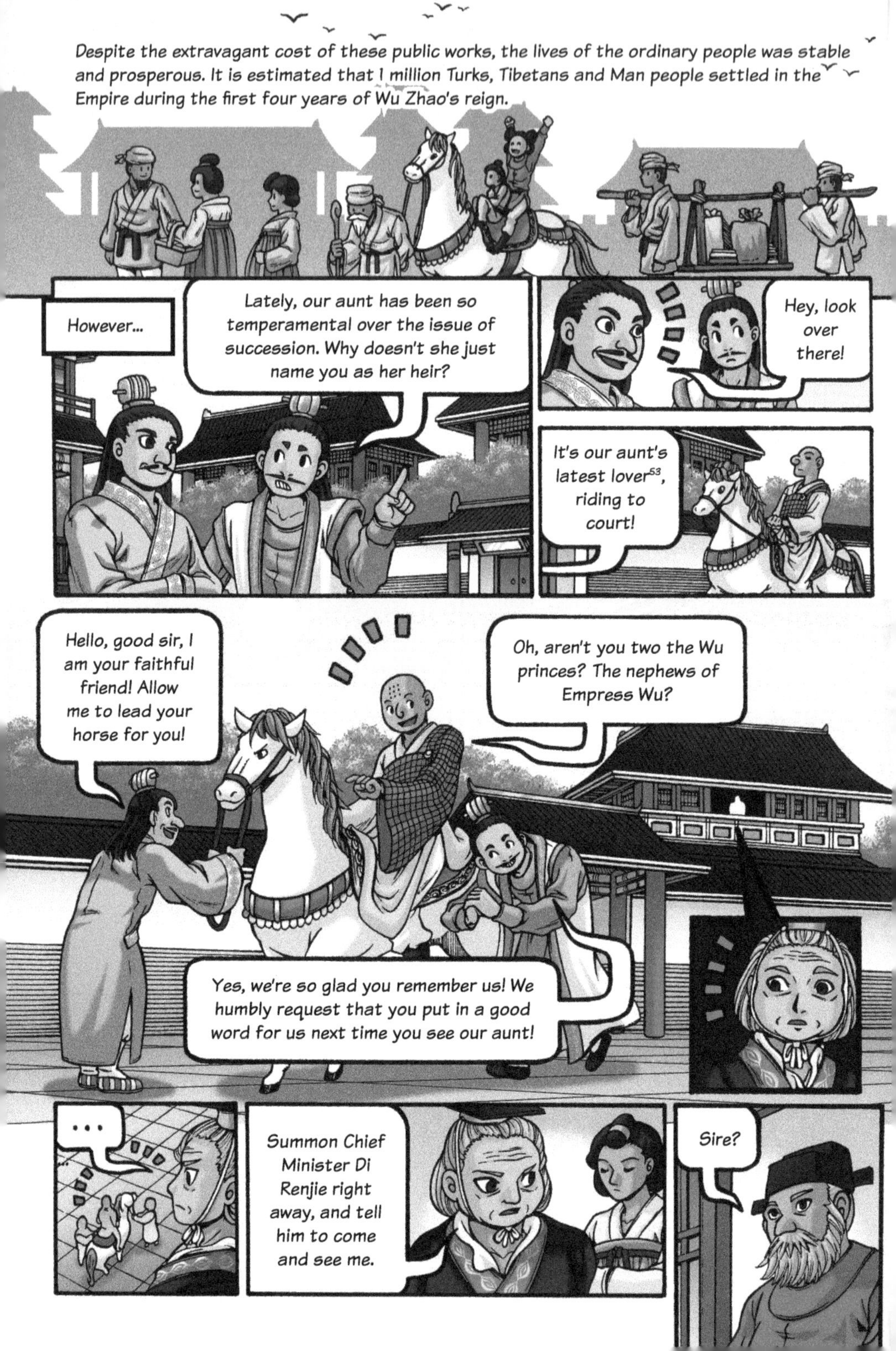

Despite the extravagant cost of these public works, the lives of the ordinary people was stable and prosperous. It is estimated that 1 million Turks, Tibetans and Man people settled in the Empire during the first four years of Wu Zhao's reign.
However...
Lately, our aunt has been so temperamental over the issue of succession. Why doesn't she just name you as her heir?
Hey, look over there!
It's our aunt's latest lover[53], riding to court!
Hello, good sir, I am your faithful friend! Allow me to lead your horse for you!
Oh, aren't you two the Wu princes? The nephews of Empress Wu?
Yes, we're so glad you remember us! We humbly request that you put in a good word for us next time you see our aunt!
...
Summon Chief Minister Di Renjie right away, and tell him to come and see me.
Sire?

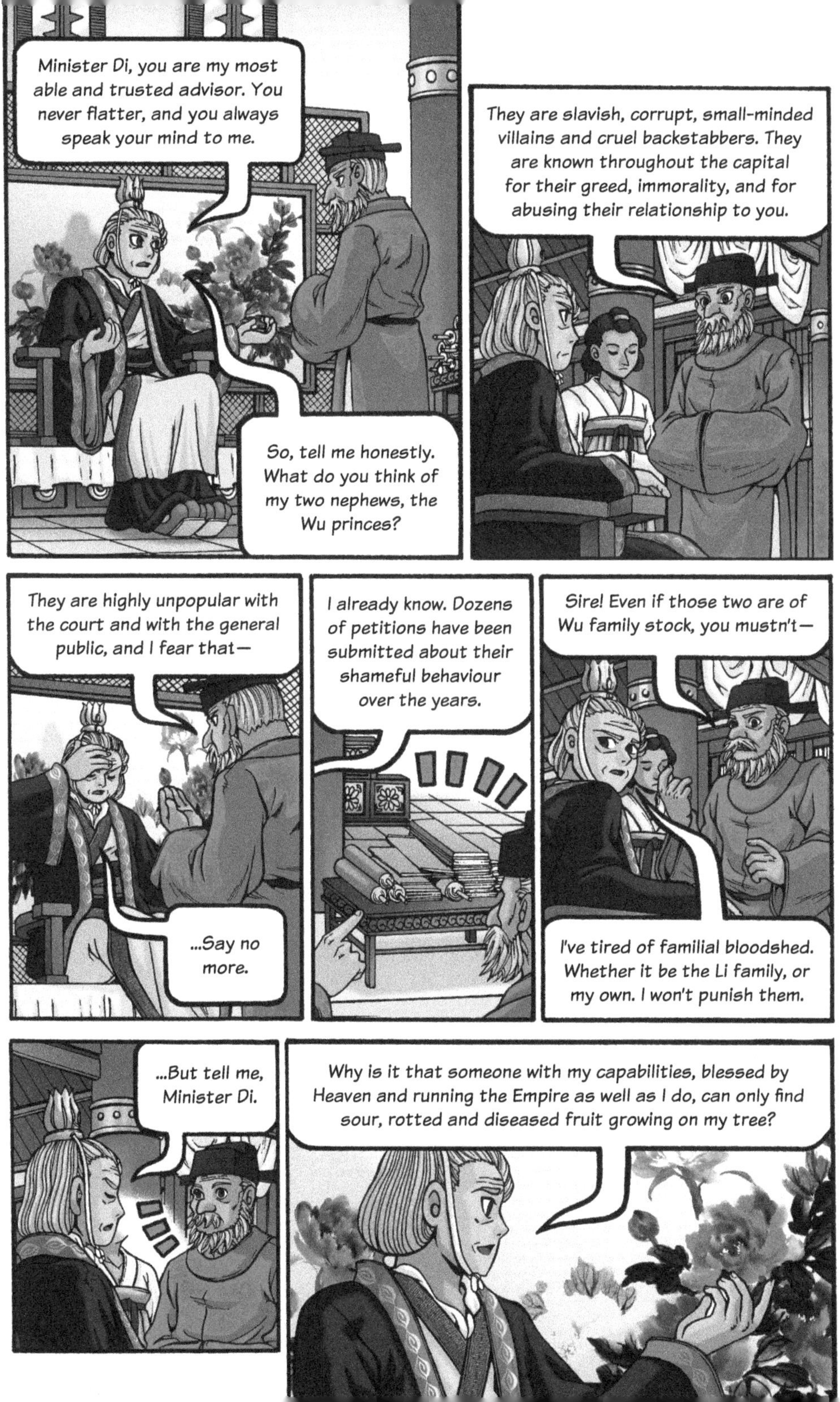
Minister Di, you are my most able and trusted advisor. You never flatter, and you always speak your mind to me.
So, tell me honestly. What do you think of my two nephews, the Wu princes?
They are slavish, corrupt, small-minded villains and cruel backstabbers. They are known throughout the capital for their greed, immorality, and for abusing their relationship to you.
They are highly unpopular with the court and with the general public, and I fear that—
...Say no more.
I already know. Dozens of petitions have been submitted about their shameful behaviour over the years.
Sire! Even if those two are of Wu family stock, you mustn't—
I've tired of familial bloodshed. Whether it be the Li family, or my own. I won't punish them.
...But tell me, Minister Di.
Why is it that someone with my capabilities, blessed by Heaven and running the Empire as well as I do, can only find sour, rotted and diseased fruit growing on my tree?

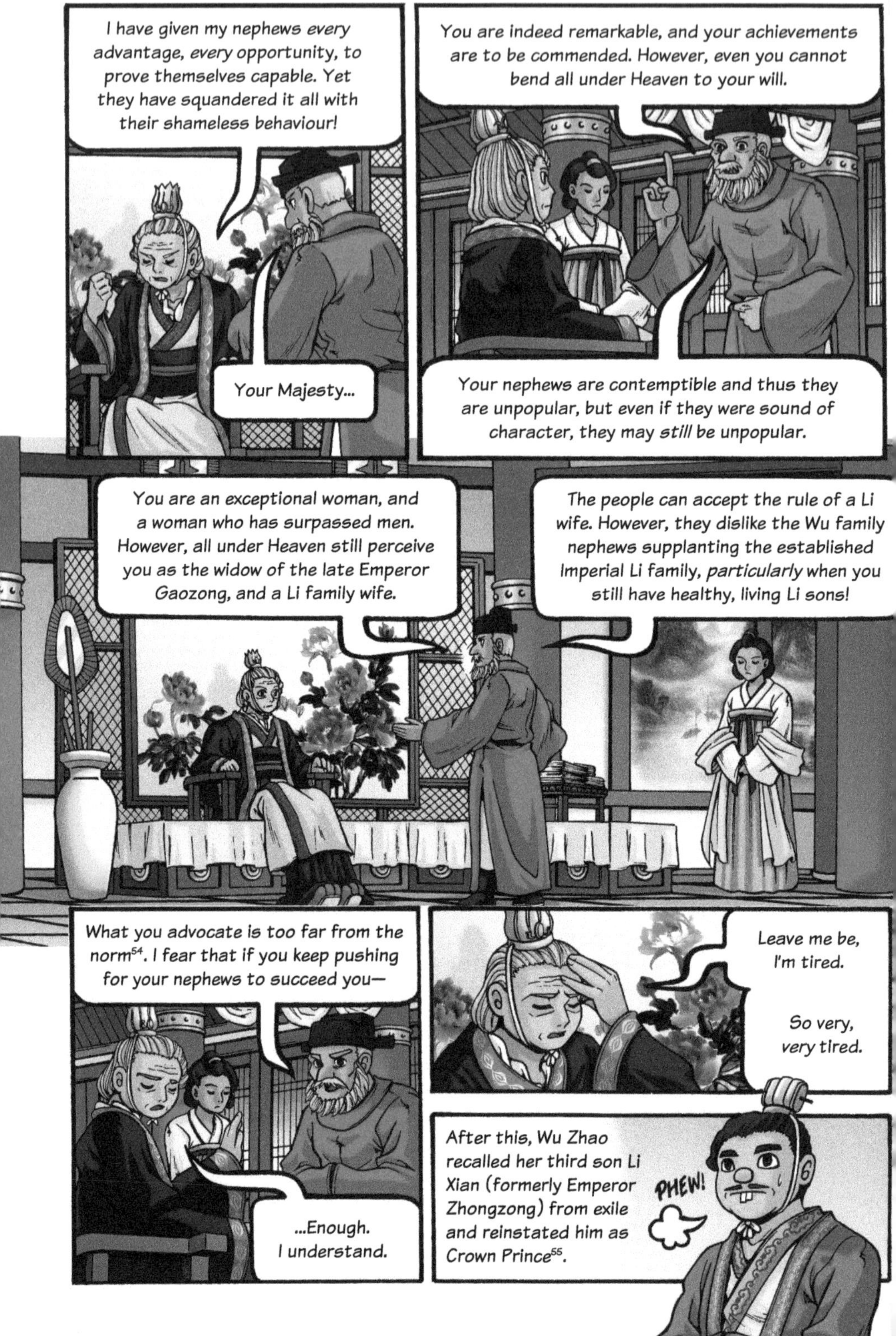
I have given my nephews *every* advantage, *every* opportunity, to prove themselves capable. Yet they have squandered it all with their shameless behaviour!
Your Majesty...
You are indeed remarkable, and your achievements are to be commended. However, even you cannot bend all under Heaven to your will.
Your nephews are contemptible and thus they are unpopular, but even if they were sound of character, they may *still* be unpopular.
You are an exceptional woman, and a woman who has surpassed men. However, all under Heaven still perceive you as the widow of the late Emperor Gaozong, and a Li family wife.
The people can accept the rule of a Li wife. However, they dislike the Wu family nephews supplanting the established Imperial Li family, *particularly* when you still have healthy, living Li sons!
What you advocate is too far from the norm[54]. I fear that if you keep pushing for your nephews to succeed you—
...Enough. I understand.
Leave me be, I'm tired.
So very, *very* tired.
After this, Wu Zhao recalled her third son Li Xian (formerly Emperor Zhongzong) from exile and reinstated him as Crown Prince[55].
PHEW!

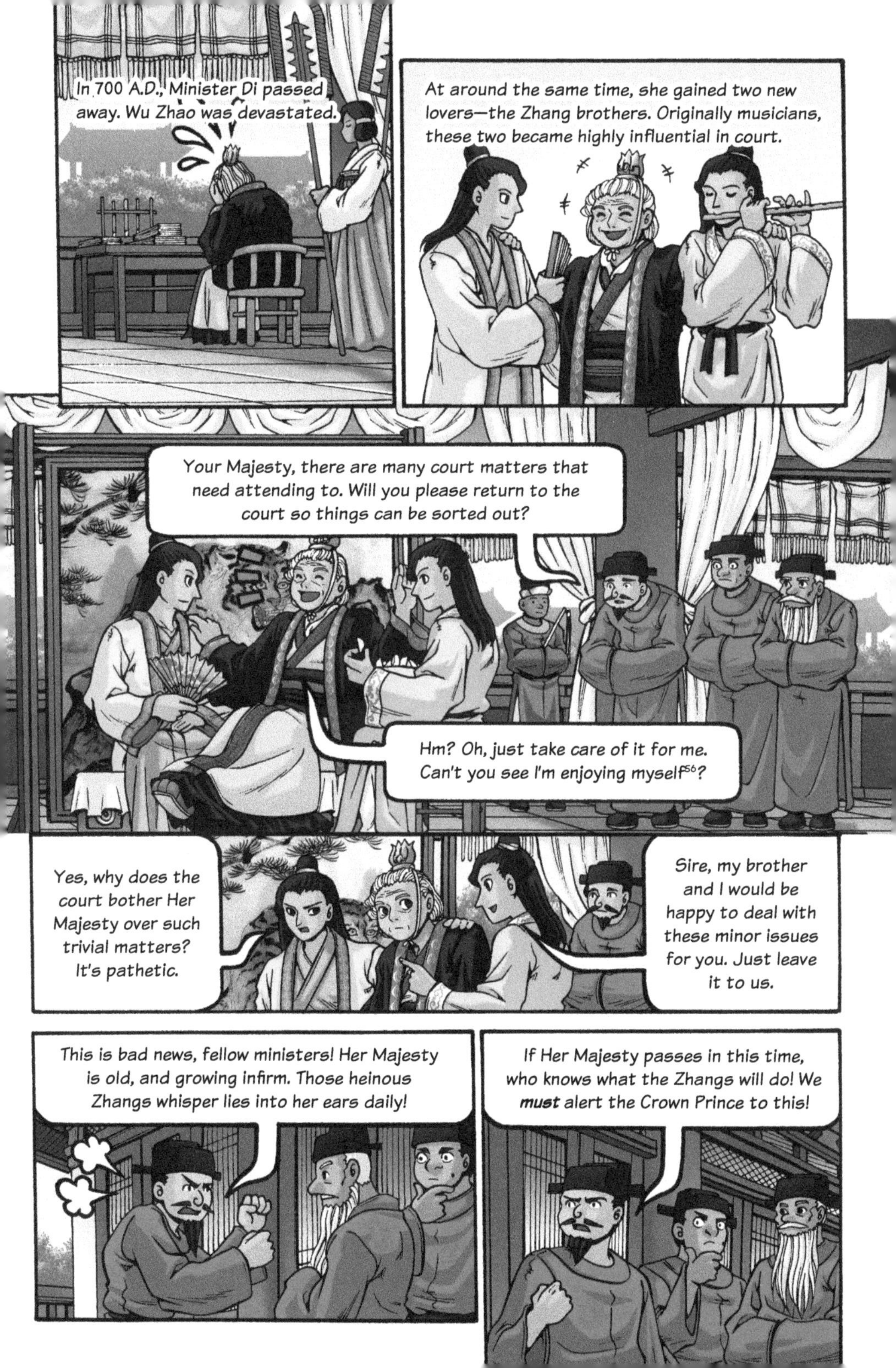
In 700 A.D., Minister Di passed away. Wu Zhao was devastated.
At around the same time, she gained two new lovers—the Zhang brothers. Originally musicians, these two became highly influential in court.
Your Majesty, there are many court matters that need attending to. Will you please return to the court so things can be sorted out?
Hm? Oh, just take care of it for me. Can't you see I'm enjoying myself[56]?
Yes, why does the court bother Her Majesty over such trivial matters? It's pathetic.
Sire, my brother and I would be happy to deal with these minor issues for you. Just leave it to us.
This is bad news, fellow ministers! Her Majesty is old, and growing infirm. Those heinous Zhangs whisper lies into her ears daily!
If Her Majesty passes in this time, who knows what the Zhangs will do! We *must* alert the Crown Prince to this!

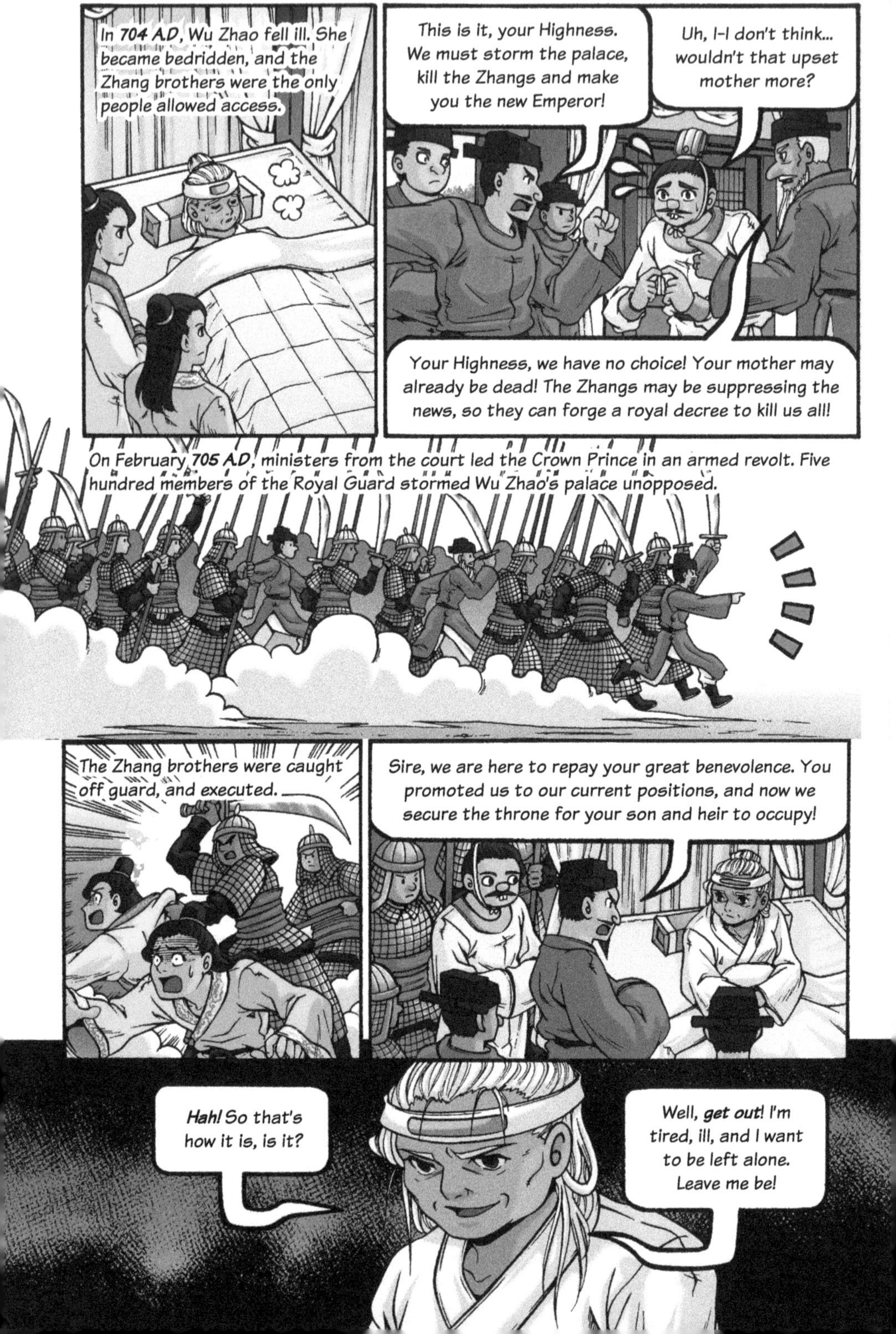
In **704 A.D**, Wu Zhao fell ill. She became bedridden, and the Zhang brothers were the only people allowed access.
This is it, your Highness. We must storm the palace, kill the Zhangs and make you the new Emperor!
Uh, I-I don't think... wouldn't that upset mother more?
Your Highness, we have no choice! Your mother may already be dead! The Zhangs may be suppressing the news, so they can forge a royal decree to kill us all!
On February **705 A.D**, ministers from the court led the Crown Prince in an armed revolt. Five hundred members of the Royal Guard stormed Wu Zhao's palace unopposed.
The Zhang brothers were caught off guard, and executed.
Sire, we are here to repay your great benevolence. You promoted us to our current positions, and now we secure the throne for your son and heir to occupy!
Hah! So that's how it is, is it?
Well, ***get out***! I'm tired, ill, and I want to be left alone. Leave me be!

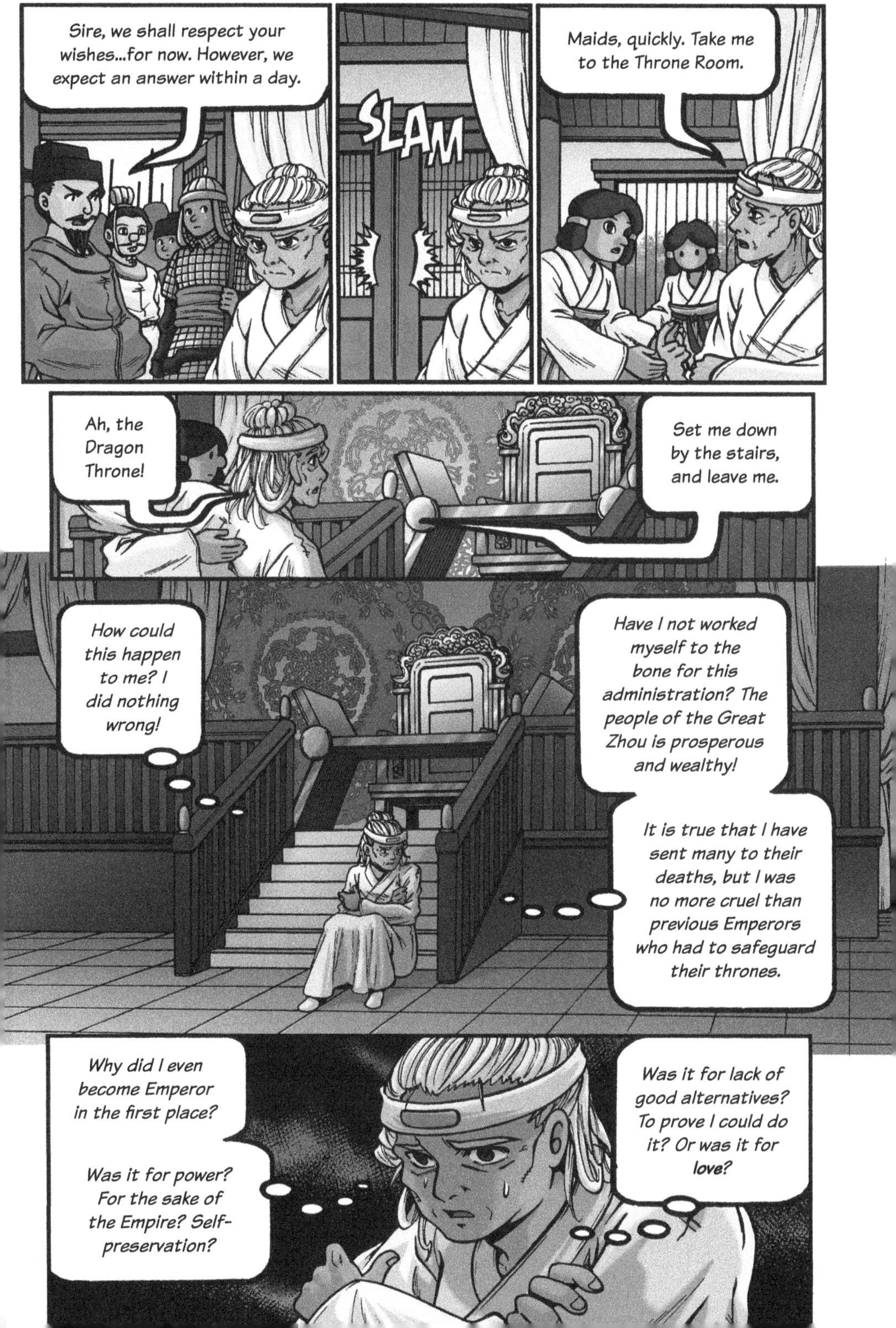
Sire, we shall respect your wishes...for now. However, we expect an answer within a day.
SLAM
Maids, quickly. Take me to the Throne Room.
Ah, the Dragon Throne!
Set me down by the stairs, and leave me.
How could this happen to me? I did nothing wrong!
Have I not worked myself to the bone for this administration? The people of the Great Zhou is prosperous and wealthy!
It is true that I have sent many to their deaths, but I was no more cruel than previous Emperors who had to safeguard their thrones.
Why did I even become Emperor in the first place?
Was it for power? For the sake of the Empire? Self-preservation?
Was it for lack of good alternatives? To prove I could do it? Or was it for **love**?

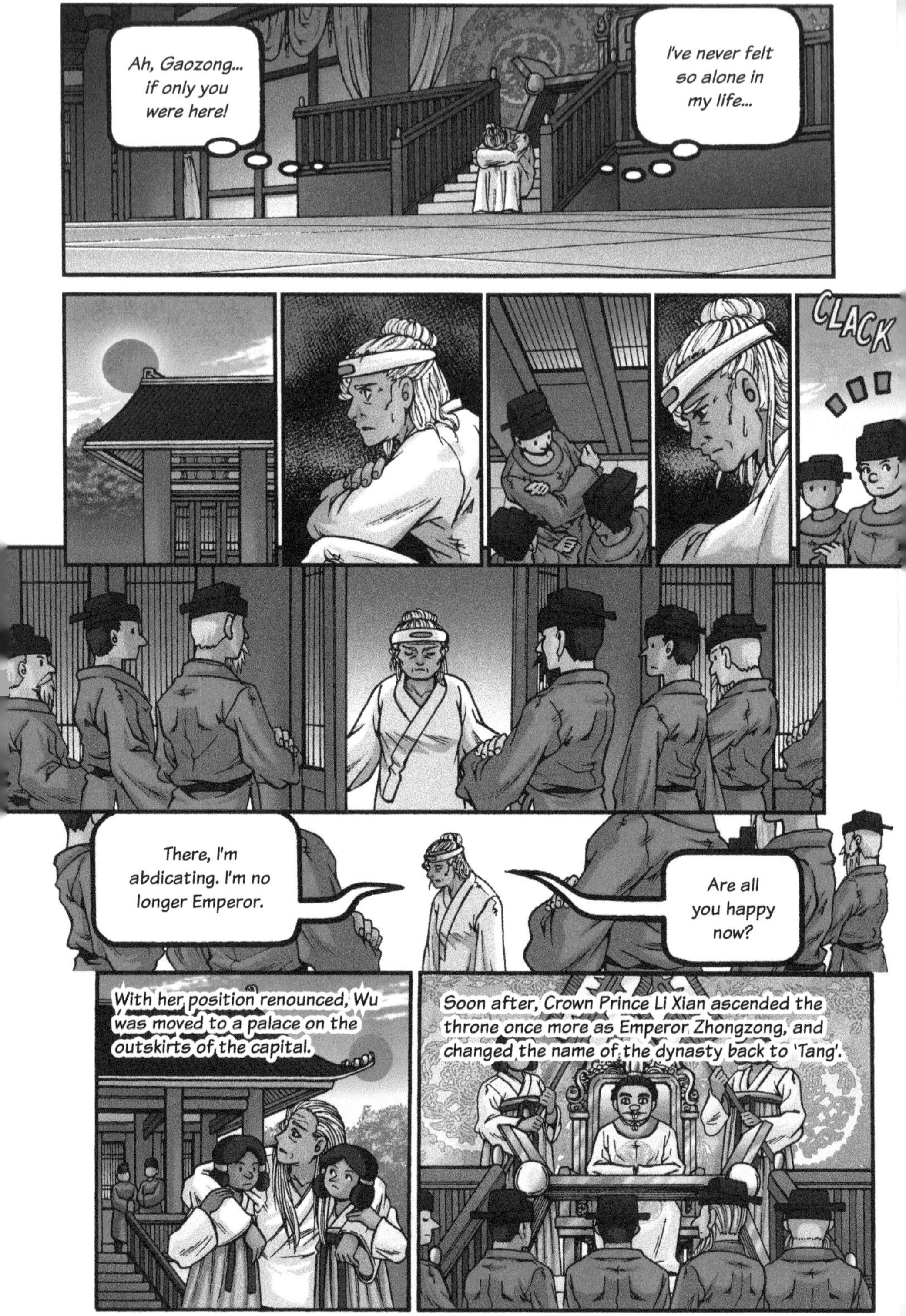
Ah, Gaozong... if only you were here!
I've never felt so alone in my life...
CLACK
There, I'm abdicating. I'm no longer Emperor.
Are all you happy now?
With her position renounced, Wu was moved to a palace on the outskirts of the capital.
Soon after, Crown Prince Li Xian ascended the throne once more as Emperor Zhongzong, and changed the name of the dynasty back to 'Tang'.

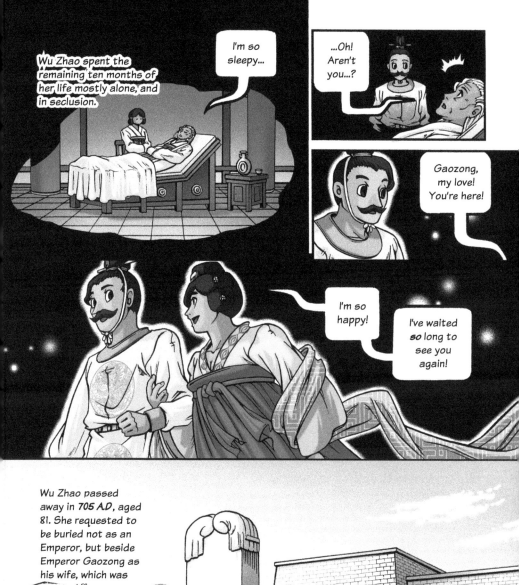

Wu Zhao spent the remaining ten months of her life mostly alone, and in seclusion.

I'm so sleepy...

...Oh! Aren't you...?

Gaozong, my love! You're here!

I'm so happy!

I've waited *so* long to see you again!

Wu Zhao passed away in **705 A.D**, aged 81. She requested to be buried not as an Emperor, but beside Emperor Gaozong as his wife, which was granted [58].

Empress Wu reigned for close to fifty years, paving the way for the most prosperous period of the Tang dynasty [59]. Posthumously, she was named "Wu Zetian", which means to "move Heaven aside"—a reference to her remarkable rule as China's sole female Emperor.

BIBLIOGRAPHY

Books
- Clements, J. (2014). "Wu: The Chinese Empress who Schemed, Seduced, and Murdered her Way to Become a Living God". Unknown: Albert Bridge Books.
- Fitzgerald, C. P. (1968). "The Empress Wu". Melbourne: Australian National University.
- Rothschild, N. H. (2008). "Wu Zhao: China's Only Woman Emperor". (P. N. Stearns, Ed.). New York: Pearson Education, Inc.
- Benn, C. (2002). "China's Golden Age: Everyday Life in the Tang Dynasty". Oxford: Oxford University Press
- Hengyu, Tian. (1997). "Wu Zetian: The Might Woman Sovereign of China". Asiapac Books: Singapore.

Journal Articles
- Rothstein-safra, R. (2017). "The Rhetoric of Transgression: Reconstructing Female Authority through Wu Zetian's Legacy". University of Central Florida.
- Song, X. (2010). "Re-gendering Chinese history: Zhao Mei's emperor Wu Zetian". East Asia, 27(4), 361–379.
- Peng, N., Yu, T., & Mills, A. (2015). "Feminist Thinking in Late Seventh-Century China: A Critical Hermeneutics Analysis of the Case of Wu Zetian". Equality, Diversity and Inclusion: An International Journal, 34(1), 67–83.
- Guisso, R. W. L., Guisso, W., & Johannesen, S. (1981). "Thunder Over the Lake: the Five Classics and the Perception of Women in Early China". Women in China: Current Directions in Historical Scholarship, 3(3), 238.
- Guisso, R. W. L. (1979). "The Reigns of the Empress Wu, Chung-Tsung and Jui-Tsung (684-712)". Sui and T'ang China, 589-906, Part I (Vol. v.3).
- Bokenkamp, S. R. (1998). "A medieval feminist critique of the Chinese world order: The case of Wu Zhao (r. 690–705)". Religion, 28(4), 383–392.
- Chen, S. (1996). "Succession Struggle and the Ethnic Identity of the Tang Imperial House". Journal of the Royal Asiatic Society, 6(3), 379-405

FOOTNOTES & ART NOTES

This book comes with a full set of footnotes and artistic sources that, due to their length, is only accessible online. Please visit the link below for the full footnotes:

www.queeniechan.com/tag/wuzetian/

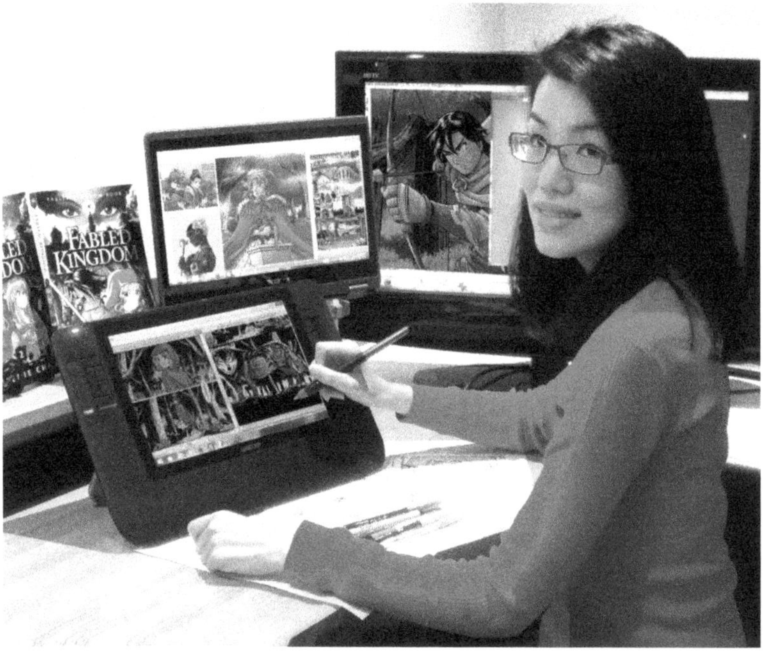
FABLED
KINGDOM

ABOUT THE CREATOR

Queenie Chan was born in Hong Kong, and migrated to Australia when she was six years old. Her first published work was *'The Dreaming'*, a mystery-horror series for LA-based publisher TOKYOPOP, which has been translated into multiple languages. She then collaborated with best-selling author Dean Koontz, and with author Kylie Chan for the prequel *'Small Shen'*. After that, she worked on several anthologies, and a 3-book fairytale-fantasy series called *'Fabled Kingdom'*.

She is currently studying a Masters of Research degree at Macquarie University, and creating a series of non-fiction children's comics about historical queens.

Please visit **www.queeniechan.com** for more information.

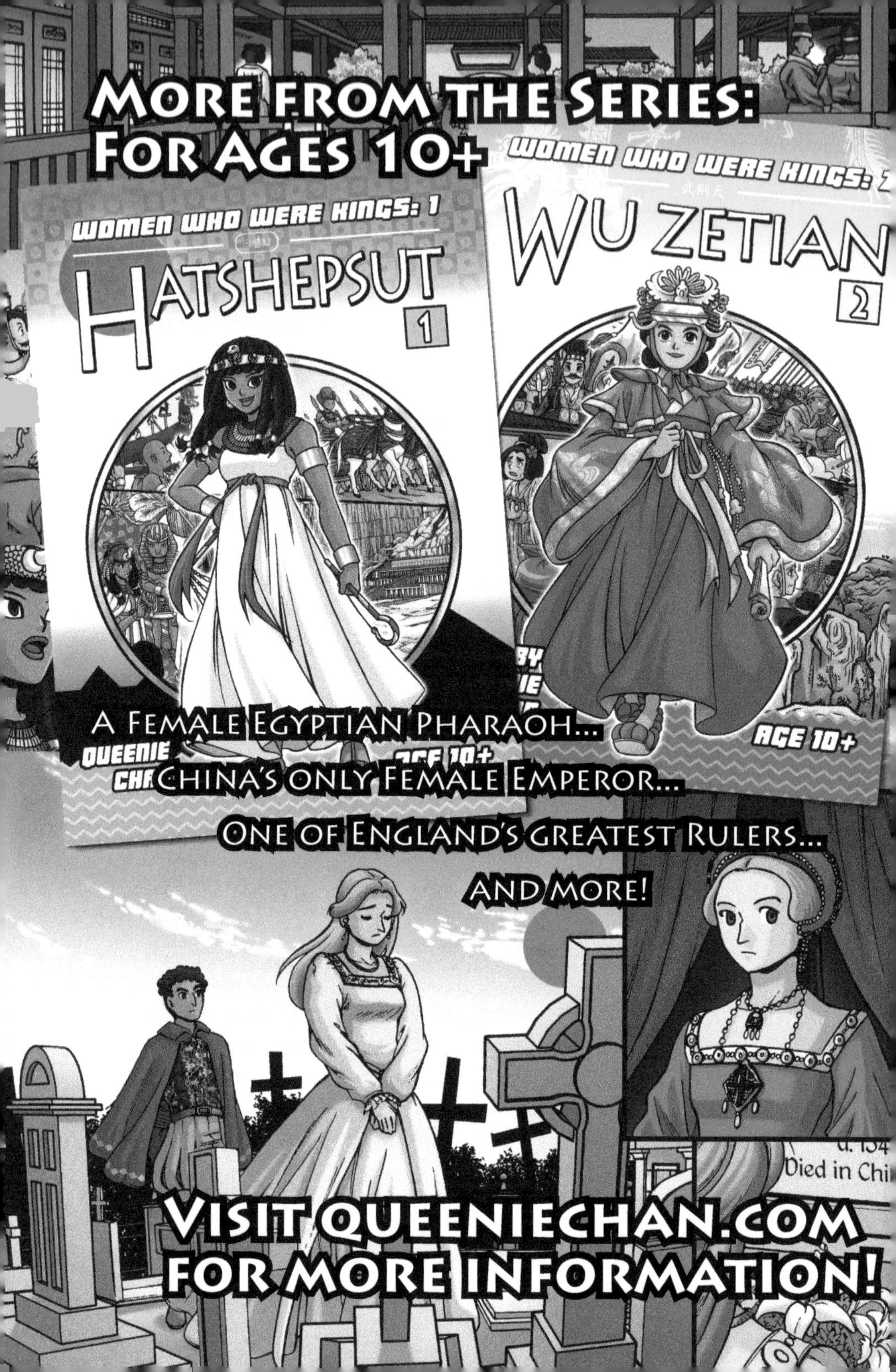
More from the Series:
For Ages 10+
WOMEN WHO WERE KINGS: 1
HATSHEPSUT
1
WOMEN WHO WERE KINGS: 2
WU ZETIAN
2
AGE 10+
A Female Egyptian Pharaoh...
China's only Female Emperor...
One of England's greatest Rulers...
And more!
Visit queeniechan.com
for more information!

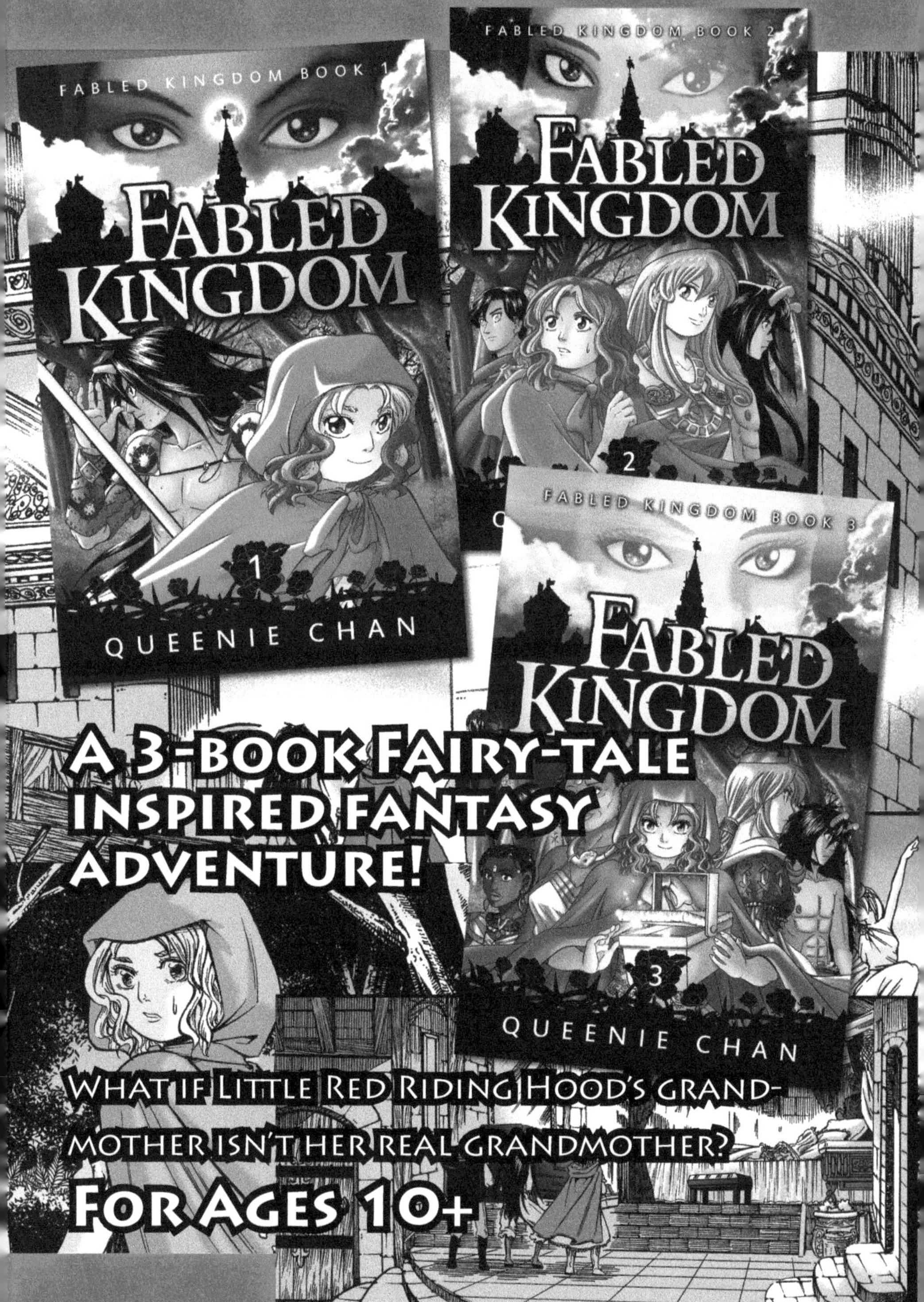
FABLED KINGDOM BOOK 1
FABLED KINGDOM
1
QUEENIE CHAN
FABLED KINGDOM BOOK 2
FABLED KINGDOM
2
FABLED KINGDOM BOOK 3
FABLED KINGDOM
3
QUEENIE CHAN
A 3-BOOK FAIRY-TALE INSPIRED FANTASY ADVENTURE!
WHAT IF LITTLE RED RIDING HOOD'S GRAND-MOTHER ISN'T HER REAL GRANDMOTHER?
FOR AGES 10+

Printed in the USA
CPSIA information can be obtained
at www.ICGtesting.com
LVHW070035070923
757475LV00042B/1400

9 781925 376081